YORK NOTES

General Editors: Professor A.N. Jef
of Stirling) & Professor Suheil Busl
University of Beirut)

Stephen Crane

THE RED BADGE
OF COURAGE

Notes by Wilson F. Engel

BA (OLD DOMINION UNIVERSITY) MA PH D (UNIVERSITY OF WISCONSIN)
Senior Analyst, Inter-National Research Institute

**LONGMAN
YORK PRESS**

YORK PRESS
Immeuble Esseily, Place Riad Solh, Beirut.

LONGMAN GROUP LIMITED
Longman House,
Burnt Mill,
Harlow,
Essex

First published 1985
ISBN 0 582 78257 0
Produced by Longman Group (FE) Ltd
Printed in Hong Kong

Contents

Part 1

Introduction

Life of Stephen Crane

Stephen Crane was born in Newark, New Jersey, on 1 November 1871, the fourteenth child of an itinerant Methodist minister. He grew up in Port Jervis, New York, received his early schooling at the Hudson River Institute at Claverack, then studied for a semester each at Lafayette College in Easton, Pennsylvania, and at Syracuse University. At Syracuse he wrote the first draft of his novel *Maggie: A Girl of the Streets*, a grim, 'naturalistic' portrayal of slum life and death. He then moved to New York City and for five years lived in poverty as a free-lance writer, doing occasional reporting for the *New York Herald* and the *New York Tribune*. The publication of *Maggie* in 1893 brought him acclaim from the best writers and editors of his time. It also brought him the friendship of the established and respected American authors Hamlin Garland (1860-1940) and William Dean Howells (1837-1920). Howells was a great champion of realism in fiction who praised realistic writers such as Tolstoy and Zola and encouraged a host of young realistic writers in America.

In 1895 Crane's great novel of the American Civil War *The Red Badge of Courage* was published in book form, having first appeared in a shorter version in newspapers. *The Red Badge of Courage* immediately became an American classic and made its author instantly famous. Even though he had never witnessed a military encounter, the book opened opportunities for him as a war correspondent. Crane is one in a long line of American writers who wrote extensively for newspapers to make a living and whose experience in writing for the masses coloured their literary style. He was hired as a correspondent for Irving Bacheller's news syndicate to cover the fighting in Cuba. On the way to Cuba, he passed through Jacksonville, Florida, where he met Cora Taylor, the proprietress of the Hotel de Dream, a brothel. Cora Taylor remained with Crane for the rest of his life. In a time of rigid morality Crane's choice of a life companion, together with his notoriously unorthodox way of living, was considered scandalous. Because of the viciousness and jealousy he encountered everywhere in America, Crane decided to live abroad. In 1897 he went to live in Surrey, England.

In England Crane became a friend of the authors Henry James

(1843-1916), H. G. Wells (1866-1946), and Joseph Conrad (1857-1924). James emigrated from America to settle in London in 1876 and to become known as a master prose stylist particularly interested in human psychology. Wells and Conrad were about to produce many of their finest works at that time. All these writers shared an international perspective and were in contact with major European literary currents.

In addition to his novels, Crane was an acknowledged master of the short story. A few of the stories he produced during the period from 1895 to 1900 are among the finest in world literature. On 1 January 1897, Crane was shipwrecked en route to Cuba. This adventure was the inspiration for the short story 'The Open Boat', the title story in *The Open Boat and Other Tales* (1898). 'The Open Boat' is an example of literary naturalism in which nature in the form of the sea is seen as hostile or at least indifferent to human tragedy.

After covering the Greco-Turkish War in 1897 and the Spanish-American War in Cuba in 1898, Crane returned in 1899 to England where he and Cora were living. He tried to rid himself of his debts by writing, but his health failed, and he died at the age of twenty-eight of tuberculosis at Badenweiler, Germany, on 5 June 1900.

In addition to *Maggie* and *The Red Badge of Courage* Crane wrote the following less successful novels: *George's Mother* (1896), *The Third Violet* (1897), *Active Service* (1899), and *The O'Ruddy* (1903; published posthumously, it was completed by Robert Barr). A collection of stories, *The Monster and Other Tales*, was published in 1899. In addition to his prose fiction, correspondence, and news reporting, Crane also produced two books of free verse anticipating twentieth-century poetry – *The Black Rider* (1895) and *War Is Kind* (1899).

The historical background

After the American Civil War (1860-5) the South, which suffered a crushing defeat, was under the tyranny of Reconstruction, a political term for rebuilding but also for punishing the rebellious southern states. The North, which won the war, was left with the many problems that always accompany the change from a wartime to a peacetime economy. But the basis of the northern states was industry, and although subject to the normal business cycles, industry gradually grew more and more prosperous during the last decades of the nineteenth century. On the other hand the basis of the southern states was agriculture dependent on slavery, an economic system that was swept away in the war. By 1877 all of the southern states were back in the Union and nominally in control of their own affairs, but their economic and social system was so badly impaired that they remained at a disadvantage for nearly eighty years.

While North and South were making painful adjustments after the Civil War, the great area offering expansion was the West. Through a vast extension of the railroads, grand new vistas were opened for settlement and agriculture. The Great Northern, the Northern Pacific, and the Union Pacific railroads opened the whole area between New York and the bountiful Northwest, and surveys carried out in California ignited the imagination of men desirous of new land and new hope. So comprehensive was the movement to settle and push forward this frontier that by 1893 the eminent historian Frederick Jackson Turner (1861-1932) could proclaim that there was no more frontier in America.

In the West the Indians were often disgracefully treated as new frontiersmen pushed into their territories. Cattle trails opened through the area, and farms covered the north central states. With the railroad, telegraph, oil and gas lighting, banks, schools, libraries, and mansions civilising the country in a very short time, the Middle West became a great agrarian power – and a political power to be reckoned with. Slaves, freed throughout the land after the Civil War, still had to become accepted as equals to whites and endured hardship and even torment until the nineteen-sixties.

As repeated economic crises – especially the Panic of 1873 involving bank and business failures – demanded new evaluations of the role of capitalism in America, the movement called Populism gave a political voice to ordinary citizens and freed men, notably to labourers and farmers. William Jennings Bryan (1860-1925), a congressman from Nebraska, became the eloquent defender of the 'little men', but he could not win the presidency. After Bryan's defeat, a reaction occurred in the 1890s against all those whose hopes had been raised by Populism. Business prospered at the expense of human rights, and industry triumphed over agrarianism.

The control of government by business meant the control of foreign policy by business. As business worked towards high tariffs to protect itself, it diverted public attention to the fortuitous revolt of Cuba against Spain. The so-called 'yellow press' of William Randolph Hearst (1863-1951) and Joseph Pulitzer (1847-1911) delighted in painting vivid pictures of atrocities in Cuba and in stirring up Americans to run to Cuba's defence. The result was the Spanish-American War (1898), which was fought 'to free Cuba', and Europe was in no position to take sides in it. The victory was a tribute to the United States Navy's preparedness – and now American imperialism was underway with Puerto Rico, the Philippines, and finally Hawaii being made possessions or territories of the United States. Theodore

('Teddy') Roosevelt (1858-1919) made his reputation during the Spanish-American War, was elected afterwards as Vice-President, and became President when William McKinley (1843-1901) was assassinated. Only then was liberal conservatism free to curb the excesses of unbridled capitalism.

Progressivism, the reform movement that grew as a response to the rapid industrialisation after the Civil War, involved work in crowded cities and especially slums by dedicated men and women. Political leaders were elected in the 1890s on progressive platforms to attack corruption and improve city life. Social workers began programmes of self-help for the poor and downtrodden. This movement had its greatest success at the state level in the late nineteenth century. Only in the early twentieth century did national legislation aimed at reform bear fruit.

In order to provide labour after the Civil War, immigrants were encouraged and came in large numbers from Europe and the Orient. Labour began to organise after the dire days of 1877, and the first unions were set up. These times were difficult not only for rough labour leaders, but for industrialists also. Herbert Spencer's *Social Statistics* (1865) made *laissez faire* (*French*, 'leave it alone') the creed of American businessmen. That meant that interference by government was considered against the best interest of business. Capitalists believed that the hard laws of economics, 'the dismal science', should determine who would be the fittest to survive and to prosper. This creed was strong until at least 1902, and it has been revived in America from time to time since then.

The minds of educated men were being transformed by a new wave of scientific thought. Charles Darwin's (1809-82) *Origin of Species* (1859) proposed that, rather than being created all at once as pictured in the biblical account, life forms had evolved through the ages. Such works as Thomas Henry Huxley's (1825-95) *Man's Place in Nature* (1863) and John Fiske's (1842-1901) *Outlines of Cosmic Philosophy* (1874) reversed the traditional views of man's supremacy in creation. Now man was seen as not privileged, but subject to the same laws of nature as the 'lower' animals. This revolution in science, affecting man's view of his place in the world, also affected his manner of dealing with others. Man was regarded as the product of a vague process known as 'natural selection'. Instead of acting out of natural nobility, man strove only to survive at all costs. Unrestrained self-interest was seen as a positive force, in tune with nature's way of weeding out weaklings through ruthless competition. Both nature and man seemed to be subject to unchangeable laws – economic, political, social laws no less than biological and physical ones.

After Chicago's Great Fire of 1871, Chicago was rebuilt to become the financial centre for the great westward expansion. Chicago became the birthplace of a truly American architecture in the work of Denkmar Adler (1844-1900), Louis Sullivan (1856-1924) and Frank Lloyd Wright (1869-1959). In architecture as in nearly all the arts, including literature, much in America had slavishly imitated European models, but the rebuilding of Chicago provided a new context for art and thought in the Middle West, from which many major figures derived both inspiration and income.

One of the most powerful forces in America in the period after the Civil War was religion, particularly the evangelical movements. Crane's father was one of thousands of Methodist preachers whose oratory roused the nation. In a time before electronic media the preachers' and politicians' speeches were, next to the newspapers, the most influential means of persuasion. Formal education was not as widespread as it is today, and those who considered themselves to be the élite of society enforced a code of morality, religion and patriotism that was an easy target for the intelligent few, such as Mark Twain (Samuel Longhorne Clemens, 1835-1910). In order to appreciate the courage it took to join the emerging realist school, it is necessary first to understand the rigidity of society and the threat that any scientific exploration, or even description, of society meant. Heroes, such as Twain's Huckleberry Finn or Crane's Henry Fleming or Maggie, flew in the face of established conventions. Realism was in fact criticism of contemporary society.

The literary background

In 1865 at the end of the Civil War many of the authors who had been famous or influential before the war were dead or had lost their influence. Dead were Washington Irving (1783-1859), James Fenimore Cooper (1789-1851), Edgar Allan Poe (1809-49), and Nathaniel Hawthorne (1804-64), to name only a few of the most influential. Herman Melville's (1819-91) great novels had all been written, and he had turned from fiction to poetry. Ralph Waldo Emerson (1803-82), the grand old man of American Transcendentalism, had produced his best-known works in the eighteen-thirties and forties. Although he still wrote and lectured, his influence was now limited. Walt Whitman (1819-92), who was the greatest literary artist to have written about the Civil War from first-hand experience, revised and added to his monumental poem *Leaves of Grass* right up to his death. But even though they remained active afterwards, Emerson, Whitman and their followers and imitators were not the main forces in literature in the post-war years. In fact, even before the war Herman Melville's *The Confidence Man: His*

Masquerade (1857) and *The Piazza Tales* (1856) signalled the end of Transcendentalism's optimism. The new literary age belonged not to Emerson and his followers, but to realists, to naturalists who saw human suffering as resulting from forces beyond man's control, and to determinists who felt that man was destined by iron laws to follow only the destiny mapped out by his heredity and environment. For determinists, free will was at best an illusion, and man was actually hemmed in on all sides by forces he could only dimly understand.

As new regions of the United States were opened to settlement after the war, so new frontiers of literature opened too. Writers depicted their own local landscapes in realistic detail. Mark Twain's *The Adventures of Huckleberry Finn* (1884), one of the finest works in American literature, evolved from his interest in humour and local colour which went back at least to Twain's comical story 'The Celebrated Jumping Frog of Calaveras County' (1865). Bret Harte (1836-1902) wrote about the new West, Sarah Orne Jewett (1849-1909) about New England, and Hamlin Garland about the prairie states. But even more important than the local colour in Garland's work was the grim reality of dehumanising economic, social, and political forces that lie beyond man's control.

Social reality was explored in novels by William Dean Howells, whose critical writings about European literature helped to mould American taste, to create interest in works by Émile Zola (1840-1902), Henrik Ibsen (1828-1906), and Leo Tolstoy (1828-1910). Howells, often called the dean of American letters during this period, was a literary mentor to Mark Twain, Hamlin Garland and Stephen Crane. The influence in America of such naturalistic writers as Émile Zola can be seen in the dark and menacing works of Frank Norris (1870-1902) and Theodore Dreiser (1871-1945). American literature, during this unusually fruitful period of assimilation of ideas, drew upon the techniques of major art movements in Europe, particularly French impressionism, and upon the ideas of the darkest theorists on the necessary implications of natural selection and the debilitating yet inevitable cycles of industrial capitalism.

Crane was familiar with and experimented with nearly all of the intellectual, literary and artistic ideas described above, and in addition he seems to have been interested in the kind of symbolism that may be found in the works of such French symbolist poets as Charles Baudelaire (1821-67) and Jean Arthur Rimbaud (1854-91). Like the noted American author and critic Henry James, whom he knew, Crane settled in southern England. He was a friend of James and of Joseph Conrad. The influence of these authors on each other's development was considerable and has not yet been adequately explored.

By the time Crane was launched on his literary career, the centre for publishing in America had shifted from Boston to New York. The shift actually took place before the Civil War, and even though Boston still had prestige, a young writer had to have assignments in New York to earn a living. Crane's versatility as a writer was largely a product of necessity. He did not have an independent income and so had to depend on his pen for making money. Newspapers had not yet become guilds with requirements of advanced degrees for admittance. Walt Whitman and Mark Twain had worked with mass media, and Crane, like them, demonstrated his talent and so was able to do occasional work. Ironically *The Red Badge of Courage* not only appeared in newspapers for the first time but gained Crane the kind of solid newspaper employment that he needed. Yet even a furious pace of production could not keep him out of debt. The quality of his later fiction suffered because of his need to write in haste.

Journalism, which fostered many famous French authors of this period, had not become formulaic. The people who bought newspapers wanted the news to be vivid and captivating, generally true but not a bare report of facts. The story that made its way into print had to have human interest. The line between this kind of journalism and the new realistic fiction was not drawn as distinctly as the line between journalism and fiction is today. Crane's 'The Open Boat' was published as a news story and then as a work of fiction, just as later Hemingway's *The Old Man and the Sea* was first a news dispatch and later a novel. Crane was in a tradition of journalists who were also novelists, and his journalism influenced the style of his novels.

Crane's formal education seems to have had very little influence on his writing. His college experience was valuable only in that it gave him the opportunity to write. More important than his brief stays at Lafayette College and Syracuse University was his self-taught manner of portraying reality vividly in a readable style. Experience seems to have lagged behind imagination in his early writings – *Maggie* and *The Red Badge of Courage* were produced before Crane had experienced either slum life or war. Later, in 'The Open Boat', the experience of being helpless in a boat on the ocean was the raw material first for a news account, then for the short story, and finally for hallucinatory dreams of the incident which Crane experienced right up to his death.

Crane belonged to a whole school of American writers whose classroom was the world, and who lived on the meagre returns for a published news feature or a short story, not on an inheritance or a foundation's grant. Melville and Whitman, Poe and Mark Twain had provided models of the rough-hewn literary professional. It is ironical but not especially surprising that when Crane turned his back on his literary achievement – a blend of imagination and experience – he failed repeatedly to produce another first-rate novel.

Relevant ideas

The American Civil War, fought from 1860 to 1865, tore the nation in two and shattered for ever the ideal of a perfectly unified nation. For decades beforehand the conflict had been brewing, precariously kept simmering by compromise, until war became inevitable. And long afterwards America felt the effects of the war socially, politically, and economically.

Documented by Walt Whitman in poetry, by Winslow Homer (1836-1910) in prints, and by Mathew B. Brady (*c*.1832-92) and his assistants in photographs, the war was finally captured, years later, in 1895, in prose fiction by Crane in his masterpiece *The Red Badge of Courage*. Perhaps distance from the agony of conflict was necessary for an imaginative approach to the psychology of a young man caught up in the gigantic struggle. Where Whitman either remains detached or focuses on his own reactions and where Homer and Brady portray external, frozen features only, Crane roams freely to capture the war on many levels. He does so without hate, yet also without total, clinical detachment. In fact, *The Red Badge of Courage* says more about the experience of war itself than about the Civil War, even though clearly it could be about no other specific conflict. Further, the distance of thirty years changed the readership for his novel, and America's view of war was now intrinsically more mythical, even romantic, just as it was about to embark on the Spanish-American War.

Although he had never been near a battlefield Crane nevertheless vividly portrayed the war that had ended six years before his birth. One facet of American realism here destroys the myth of experience as the only true source of artistic inspiration. Yet Crane's experience of the Civil War was in some respects deeper than that of the participants themselves, and, of all the monuments of that war, his is supreme in its impact.

The breakdown of Transcendentalism began well before the Civil War, but romantic idealism is difficult to suppress for long. Emerson, Thoreau, and a host of other authors felt that behind the façade of ordinary experience lay a greater, more transcendent reality. They thought that man's imaginative experience of that transcendent reality was his triumph and fulfilment: nature allowed man access to the depths of his own being, and nature's laws were ultimately designed to ennoble man. With some roots in German and English Romanticism and some in a 'native' religious movement, Transcendentalism became a kind of secular religion. In opposition to this movement was the emergence of empiricism, or basing judgments on experience, particularly experience of the rough edges of life.

After witnessing the break-up of national unity, Americans no longer felt comfortable with the idea that nature was a blessed and benevolent spirit that was naturally kind to men who were receptive to her. Now the reality of personal experience, not just vivid imaginings, tested and shaped the character of man. Henry Fleming, the hero of *The Red Badge of Courage*, constantly turns from idealism to its negation in experience and back again, and he serves as a literary symbol of the shift from Emersonian idealism to pragmatism on the one hand and to nationalism on the other.

Many literary currents carried the new concern for realism in different directions. For example, the critical theory of the late nineteenth-century literary movement called naturalism assumed that life could be presented scientifically in prose. Émile Zola's influential essay *Le Roman expérimental* (1880) demonstrates that the novelist, like the scientist, should observe and analyse life, particularly its sordid aspects, to discover the laws or 'natural' forces that lie behind phenomena of social existence. A whole school of French naturalism sprang up which included Zola, the brothers Edmond and Jules de Goncourt (1822-96; 1830-70) and Guy de Maupassant (1850-93). From them English naturalists such as George Moore (1852-1933) and George Gissing (1857-1903) drew inspiration. Stephen Crane, Theodore Dreiser, Frank Norris, and James T. Farrell (1904-79) were among American writers influenced in part by the naturalists. This movement was widespread, affecting not only the novel but drama and the visual arts also. It was a necessary corrective to the artificiality of a decayed idealism. While it is appropriate to associate Crane with the naturalists when discussing a few of his works, notably *Maggie* and 'The Open Boat', Crane's genius was greater than the confines of one literary movement, however complete its tenets may seem.

Determinism was another literary current, related in some respects to naturalism, yet more bound to the darker theories of economists and social scientists than naturalism. Where naturalists, according to Zola, sought to discover laws, determinists began with the premise that the laws of nature were everywhere in evidence and everywhere destructive to man. The dominating philosophy behind many works by Norris, Dreiser, and even Zola, determinism meant that a man's entire course of life was determined by factors he could not control even if he were aware of them. Character is bound by iron laws of heredity and environment. Free will is simply an illusion within this framework. Man is caught in a miserable trap and cannot escape until his merciful death.

A third influential literary movement, symbolism, emerged as a reaction to naturalism in France in the late nineteenth century. Rather than dwelling on the myriad details of sordid reality, symbolists concentrated on the imagination as an equivalent to reality. Rather than stating anything directly, symbolists expressed themselves obliquely through symbols woven in a fabric of densely packed powerful images. The great figure in this movement, the poet Baudelaire, influenced other poets like Paul Verlaine (1844-96), Stéphane Mallarmé (1842-98), Rimbaud, and Jules Laforgue (1860-87). Symbolism had a profound influence on world literature, art, and music. One of the major contributions of the symbolists was the almost exclusive use of free verse in poetry, making poetry a near-equivalent to prose. The later movements of imagism and decadence stemmed directly from the symbolists. Crane's prose style and his use of symbols both owe something to this movement.

The influence of photography on the literary realists has long been acknowledged, and the photographs produced by Brady and his associates of the American Civil War coloured the public's conception of what the soldiers and battles looked like. But the influence of the photographs was more than just documentary in nature. The objective point of view, the hazy atmosphere, and the grim and grisly realism of the subject matter are mirrored in the work of Whitman and Crane. But literature not only imitated photography, it competed with the new medium by suggesting levels of imaginative experience that could not be seen through a camera's lens. Crane's *The Red Badge of Courage* is the moving picture that might have been taken of the inside of Henry Fleming's mind, if a camera had that capability.

Another medium also experimented with light during this period and left its mark on the other media just as photography did – painting. Impressionism, the late nineteenth-century movement in French painting, was based on a theory of light. The theory was complex, but basically it stated that areas of colour interact with one another to form a recognisable image. What might at close range be small pools of colour only, farther back would become a shimmering image. Crane's use of colours and hazy images links *The Red Badge of Courage* to this movement, one of whose leaders was Claude Monet (1840-1926).

The Red Badge of Courage belongs to one of the most popular genres or kinds of novel – the *Bildungsroman*, or novel of character development. The model for this kind of novel is *Wilhelm Meisters Lehrjahre* (*The Apprenticeship of Wilhelm Meister*, 1796), by the German author Johann Wolfgang von Goethe (1749-1832). This kind of novel has had a virtually immeasurable impact upon American literature, since the best of American writing tends to be based on the collision of a single man with the complexities of the external world. This genre, which has roots deep in Western literary tradition, allowed the reader to follow the development of a young figure (usually male, but not always) as disillusionment affects and forms character.

Methodism was the faith preached by Crane's father, and one of Crane's more sensitive critics irrepressibly calls Crane a 'preacher's kid'. But Crane does not wear Methodism – the teachings of John Wesley (1703-91) and his followers – on his sleeve. In fact, Crane is more a cultural than a theological Methodist, and he often decried the hypocrisy he discerned in the outwardly pious and seemingly devout. Crane led an unorthodox life, and most Methodists would have been scandalised by his association with Cora. Yet in his writing he does not go out of his way to criticise religion. Harold Frederic (1856-98), who wrote *Theron Ware* as a direct attack on Methodism, is by no means a Stephen Crane. Crane's Methodism, if that is what it must be called, is a sympathetic apprehension of his fellow man and of the potential symbolic overtones in nature that may or may not be coloured by man's vivid imaginings. It is a searching for meaning when the conditions for judgment are constantly changing. Crane's refusal to judge or condemn, while at the same time refusing to release his hero from feelings of guilt and remorse or to allow his hero the easy solution of a formulaic faith, possibly springs from his religious roots. A full analysis of Methodism's impact on American literature needs to be undertaken, and Crane deserves a chapter in that study.

A note on the text

The first American edition of *The Red Badge of Courage* was published by Appleton and Company in New York in 1895. Two manuscript versions, a short draft and a long draft, were bound by Crane and sent to his close friend Willis Brooks Hawkins in January 1896 as a gift. Pages missing from this bound collection in manuscript have been found at a number of libraries. The bound collection itself is in the Clifton Waller Barrett Crane Collection at the University of Virginia. Most student editions are based on the first American edition with notes showing changes and deletions from the manuscripts. But beware: editions vary considerably. (A list of editions will be found in Part 5, 'Suggestions for further reading'.)

Part 2

Summaries
of THE RED BADGE OF COURAGE

A general summary

Henry Fleming, a Union Army soldier, joined the army dreaming of heroic acts but now wonders whether he will have the courage to stand and fight in battle or whether he will run away. His friend Jim Conklin and the other soldiers do not seem to share his doubts and fears. Finally in his first battle, Fleming does run, and in his shame and perplexity seeks out a wooded area far from battle. The sight of a grisly corpse drives him back to humanity. He joins a straggling group of wounded and maimed men, one of whom is his friend Jim Conklin. After watching Conklin die and after abandoning a wretched tattered man, Fleming decides to rejoin his own regiment. A man clubs him with his rifle butt so that he can hardly walk, and a faceless man guides him back to his unit. Fleming is welcomed back since none of his comrades suspects that he was a coward. His lie about being shot in the head is generally believed, and his bandage with its blood stains becomes a symbol of courage, not cowardice. Wilson, a soldier who nurses him, has been changed by his war experience, and becomes Henry Fleming's friend and fellow-hero as the action progresses. Now when the unit goes into battle, Fleming becomes the model fighting man. His lieutenant praises him, and the two together lead the men into battle. Fleming takes over from the colour-bearer who is killed, and he makes an heroic figure with his flag and his bloody bandages. Finally Fleming and Wilson lead a devastating charge, and rout the Confederate soldiers entirely. For this they receive general acclaim. As the army moves on, Fleming thinks about the many changes he has endured. His guilty feelings about leaving the tattered man give him humility to temper his pride in his new role as hero.

Detailed summaries

Chapter 1

A tall soldier, later identified as Jim Conklin, excites his fellow Union soldiers with a rumour that they will soon break camp to engage the enemy. A loud-voiced private, later identified as Wilson, disputes the information, while a youthful private, the impressionable Henry Fleming, withdraws into his hut to think. In his meditation the young private reviews his early enthusiasm for joining the army and his mother's resistance to the idea. He enlisted secretly, then told his mother, who sadly resigned herself to his departure. After having been given a hero's send-off by his village and by strangers along the railway, he fell in step with the seemingly endless routine of military life and wondered if he would ever see a battle. He also wondered whether he would run when faced with the enemy, concluding for the moment that he would know how courageous he was only when the test came. When Jim Conklin enters the hut, Henry asks him first whether any of the men will run from battle and then whether Jim himself will run. Jim's commonsense answers comfort Henry for a while.

NOTES AND GLOSSARY:

tall soldier: Jim Conklin, first identified like most of the characters only by description; see Chapter 9 for his death

blue-clothed men: soldiers of the Union Army of the North, whose uniforms were blue

teamster: driver of a team; here of a team of mules or horses

the loud one: Wilson, who, like Henry Fleming, develops as a character in the novel; see Chapters 14 and following for the change in him

youthful private: Henry Fleming, through whose eyes and mind most of the action is seen

illustrated weekly: illustrated with engravings, these newspapers had wide popular appeal

thought-images: Fleming's imaginative mind forms images easily

Greeklike struggle: like the heroic battles of the ancient Greeks

Homeric: as in Homer's *Odyssey* and *Iliad*, both probably composed before 700BC, where fierce individual heroism was a major theme

church bell: a symbol and the means of bringing Fleming to his decision to enlist

quilt: bed cover

returning with his shield or on it: like the ancient Spartans, for whom cowardice in battle (throwing down the shield to flee) was an unforgivable crime, and death in battle (with the body carried home afterwards on the shield) the highest honour

hull: (*American dialect*) whole

knet: (*American dialect*) knitted

licker: (*American dialect*) liquor

kin:	(*American dialect*) can
dern:	(*American dialect*) darn
allus:	(*American dialect*) always
a-learning:	(*archaic-illiterate*) teaching
blue demonstration:	show of military force by the Union Army
reviewed:	paraded
pickets:	troops sent out to watch for the approach of the enemy or his scouts
dum:	dumb
gray . . . hordes:	soldiers of the Confederate or Rebel Army of the South, who wore grey uniforms
Huns:	Asiatic warlike nomads who under their famous ruler Attila overran and ravaged a great part of Continental Europe (AD441-53)
holt:	(*American dialect*) hold
haversack:	stout canvas bag worn with a strap over the shoulder in which a soldier carried his day's rations
Fresh fish!:	derisive nickname for new, untried soldiers
mathematically prove:	prove by reasoning what ought to happen in battle without or before experiencing it
hull kit-and-boodle:	everyone
all-to-oncet:	(*illiterate*) all at once
scrimmages:	skirmishes
Be jiminey:	euphemism for the oath 'By God!'

Chapter 2

The rumour of battle proving false, Henry has time to brood about his problems. Riddled with doubts and fears about how he will do in battle, he wonders about his comrades, who all seem composed, and not at all worried. Are they heroes, or are they all full of dark questions? The waiting is nearly intolerable, but at last the regiment is on the march. The soldiers seem full of laughter; one fat soldier tries to steal a horse but is driven off by a young girl. In the evening Henry wishes he were back at home. By firelight he discusses the situation with Wilson, who is all confidence. He says he will not run under any circumstances. Henry sleeps, dreaming visions of a thousand-tongued fear.

NOTES AND GLOSSARY:

chemist:	Henry suggests here that no man can predict 'mathematically' whether he will run from a battle – only the 'chemistry' of the actual test in battle will decide whether a man is courageous

colonel: superior officer of a regiment
brigades: subdivisions of an army, usually consisting of two regiments
regiments: considerable bodies of troops unified under one command, usually the largest fighting unit
crows and catcalls: derisive, taunting bird and animal cries
implike: like little evil spirits
getting blue: becoming dejected
about every clip: nearly every engagement
rations: field rations of food
Gee rod!:   euphemism for 'Jesus God!', an oath
skedaddled: (*US military slang,* introduced during the Civil War) fled
Napoleon Bonaparte: (1769-1824) Emperor of France
thousand-tongued fear: the traditional image of rumour with its many tongues has become an image of fear
'I'll bid five':   possibly the soldiers are playing the card game poker

---

Chapter 3

The regiment continues to move on. Unneeded supplies are cast by the trail. The regiment becomes more efficient than it had been. One morning Henry finds himself boxed in a mass of moving men, and suddenly they are formed up for battle. Moving toward the fighting, the men encounter the body of a dead soldier. Henry is upset and even considers warning his comrades about the danger ahead. The men dig in, then move and dig in again. They are grumbling that they are not taking part in the battle. Finally they move within sight of the firing rifles of the enemy. The loud soldier surprises Henry by giving him a packet done up in a yellow envelope. This loud, complaining man fears that he will die in the coming engagement.

NOTES AND GLOSSARY:
pontoon bridges: bridges supported by floating vessels
routed out: turned out of bed
color-bearer: soldier assigned to carry the flag or 'colours'
moving box: symbol of Henry's feeling of confinement and helplessness in a situation he cannot control
girted: girded
body of a dead soldier: symbol of death repeated with variations throughout the book; compare Chapter 7
the Question: possibly 'What lies beyond death?' but left unspecific

blood-swollen god: like Mars or Enyo, war gods of antiquity, represented as blood-thirsty giants who delight in devouring men and gore on battlefields

cathedral light of the forest: Crane's use of religious language to show the symbolic aspect of nature, is repeated throughout the book

engineering feat . . . grandmother: humorous comparison

little packet . . . yellow envelope: symbol of Wilson's fear that he will die; compare Chapter 15 where he retrieves the envelope from Fleming

Chapter 4

The brigade halts on the fringe of a grove. Rumours about what is happening in the battle fly about. The reality of battle with its sounds and threats comes to the men. The youth's lieutenant is wounded in the hand, and the captain helps him to bind the wound. The men withdrawing from the battle impress the youth with their confusion and their determination to flee. Fleming decides that he might indeed run, but that he must see the enemy first.

NOTES AND GLOSSARY:

304th: no such regiment existed, though a 34th did

bushwhacker: a guerilla fighter, on the Confederate side

kentry: (*American dialect*) country

disregardless: regardless

storm banshee . . . . banshee shrieks: in Irish and Scottish folklore, a banshee is a supernatural being in the shape of an old woman who foretells death by her wailing

Chapter 5

As Henry waits for the enemy to appear, he remembers waiting for a circus parade in his home town. The enemy soldiers suddenly appear and a general urges the colonel to hold back the charge at all costs. Fleming unconsciously throws his rifle into firing position toward the enemy and begins working it like a machine. He is wholly absorbed in his work and only notices a few details aside from it. One man tries to flee but is urged back by the lieutenant. Others fall on all sides, wounded or dead. The enemy withdraws, and the men are exultant. Henry surveys the battlefield – the contorted dead, the wounded limping to the rear, the guns still firing. He notices that the battle has spread far and wide. He also notices that nature seems to be unaffected by the fight.

NOTES AND GLOSSARY:

old fellow . . . cracker box: symbol of detached, critical observation intended to draw attention to oneself

as if . . . new bonnets: feminine image of a new regiment here engaged in battle for the first time; a ludicrous and pathetic sight

pommeling: beating with the pommel or knob on the hilt of a sword

pow-wow: ceremony of American Indians with magic and chanting to conjure success in war

Chapter 6

Henry Fleming thinks that he has passed the test of battle. He is very pleased with himself, and so are his fellow soldiers. But then another charge of Confederate soldiers bears down upon them, and they are all discouraged. All around the youth men turn to run. Feeling that a general retreat is beginning, he turns back. He runs past his lieutenant, who threatens him, and then blindly runs to the rear. He thinks he understands the situation better than anyone else, and he feels that all those still fighting are fools. When he comes upon the general and his staff, he hears that the regiment has held the enemy back.

NOTES AND GLOSSARY:

temple of this god: the war god

chant a paean: sing a song of triumph

Chapter 7

Henry is stung by the realisation that he has been proved wrong, and he feels betrayed. He remembers his comrades who held the enemy back and wonders what they will say if he ever returns. Ashamed, he retreats to a thick wood, penetrates the wood to its inmost recesses, and enters a chapel-like area. There he is horrified to see a long-dead man gazing at him, with ants running about his face. Afraid to turn his back on the dead man, Henry backs off, then runs frantically away. He remembers the greedy ants as he reaches new regions of natural beauty.

NOTES AND GLOSSARY:

no philosopher of his race: of course, the squirrel that runs when Henry frightens it, does not pause to reflect on why he does so; he is governed by instinct

boughs . . . chapel: a symbolic consecrated spot in the wood, with death as its abiding spirit

| soughingly: | as if sighing or murmuring |
| edifice: | imposing building |

Chapter 8

After a deep silence when all noise seems to have stopped everywhere, the guns begin to boom again. This time Henry runs towards the battle. He needs to see the actual conflict producing corpses in its machine-like way. He meets a stream of men who are wounded and maimed and joins them. Among the various wounded and dying men is a tattered man, who strikes up a conversation with Henry, but when he asks where Henry's wound is, the youth avoids him for shame.

NOTES AND GLOSSARY:

a-struggle:	(*archaic*) struggling
forlorn hopes:	translation of *enfants perdus (French*, literally 'lost children'), advance troops placed in a hopelessly dangerous position
spectral soldier:	Henry does not immediately recognise Jim Conklin, who has received a mortal wound
tattered man:	the tattered man becomes a symbol of Henry's lack of charity
mebbe:	(*American dialect*) maybe
fit:	(*American dialect*) fought

Chapter 9

Henry feels guilt and shame because he does not have a wound, a 'red badge of courage'. The spectral soldier's sufferings attract Henry's attention, and he realises that the man is Jim Conklin, who in turn recognises him. Jim announces that he has been shot and that he most fears being run down by the headlong rush of artillery wagons. Henry promises to protect him, and he takes him out of the road when a battery rushes through. In a field, Jim insists that he be let alone, then, seeming to find the spot he wants, falls down dead.

NOTES AND GLOSSARY:

red badge of courage: a major symbol; a wound means courage and not flight

passion of his wounds: extreme suffering, with overtones of the Passion of Jesus Christ

helitywhoop:	with a noise like the creatures of hell
tech:	(*American dialect*) touch
hornpipe:	lively and vigorous sailors' dance
philippic:	an oration of invective

red sun . . . wafer: a powerful image relating nature (the sun) to the Christian rite of Holy Communion (wine-dipped wafer)

Chapter 10

The tattered man joins Fleming over Jim's corpse, and he advises Henry to rejoin the living. He describes how his neighbour Tom Jamison first noticed that he was wounded. Then he was wounded again, and here he was with small children at home depending on him. He warns Henry that his wound may be worse than he thinks. When he asks where Henry's wound is, Henry becomes very rude and flees from him. The tattered man then becomes delirious and speaks as if to Tom Jamison. He wanders helplessly into a field. Henry Fleming now wishes he were dead since someone like the tattered man is sure to dredge up the fact that he had run from battle.

NOTES AND GLOSSARY:

jim-dandy:	fine fellow
Nary:	(*colloquial*) not ever
ol' number one:	oneself
swad:	(*American slang*) mass or crowd
bella:	(*American dialect*) bellow
skeared:	(*American dialect*) scared
cotch:	(*American dialect*) caught

Chapter 11

Rounding a hillock, Henry Fleming sees a general retreat. Against the tide of fearful men and supplies, new lines of soldiers are thrusting forward towards the battle. He wishes he were made of the same stuff as they are. He now desires to join the war again, but he has no rifle and despairs of finding his regiment in all the confusion. Even if he could find it, what would the men say? And he does not have an heroic disposition. Hungry and thirsty and beginning to see spots before his eyes, he despairs of being anything but a coward, yet he is drawn to the battlefield. Ironically if he could find his army defeated, he would be vindicated, but if his army is winning, he would be lost forever. Yet the Union Army would surely win. He tries to imagine what he would say and what derision he would meet when he returned.

NOTES AND GLOSSARY:

flying high . . . wings of war: like Icarus of the ancient Greek story, who, with his ingenious father Daedalus, escaped from the labyrinth of King Minos of Crete on wings

of feathers and wax, but who flew too near the sun and, his waxen wings melting, fell to drown in the sea
mothlike quality: as a moth is attracted to the deadly flame
Henry Fleming: the first mention of his full name

Chapter 12

As soon as the reinforcements disappear towards the battle front, soldiers emerge again in panicked flight. Henry forgets himself in a desperate urge to find out what has happened. As the men speed wildly by, Fleming grabs one by the arm to ask a question, but the man brings down the butt of his rifle onto Henry's head. Dazed by the blow, Henry struggles to keep his senses. The scene becomes confused. Destruction is everywhere. Fleming's wound is almost unbearable. A cheery voice rings out offering aid. The owner of the cheery voice magically escorts him back to the 304th Regiment and departs. Fleming realises that he has not seen the man's face.

NOTES AND GLOSSARY:
man wrestling with a creature of the air: like Jacob wrestling with the angle in the Bible, Genesis 32: 24
ruck: quantity
owner of the cheery voice: marks the transition to selfless actions that characterise the second half of *The Red Badge of Courage*
Johnnies: Johnny Rebs, or Confederate soldiers
gamin: street urchin

Chapter 13

Henry Fleming is almost too tired and hurt to invent a lie as he returns to his own regiment. Wilson, the sentry for the night, recognises his voice. As they talk, Henry says he has been shot in the head. Corporal Simpson helps Henry to Wilson's bed, examines his wound, and goes to have Wilson relieved so that he might help Henry. Henry meanwhile sits by the fire observing the various attitudes of the men asleep all around. Wilson soaks a handkerchief he has taken from his pocket and ties it around Henry's wounded head. Then he lays out his blankets for Henry to sleep in, and, too tired to argue for long about this selfless charity, Henry falls asleep.

NOTES AND GLOSSARY:
toddy-stricken: having drunk liquor, hot water and sugar and spice ('hot toddy')

Chapter 14

When he awakens in the morning, Henry imagines the sleeping soldiers around him as dead, but soon shakes off his fear by interpreting his vision as prophecy. Then, on command, the regiment rises for breakfast. Henry notices that Wilson has become attentive to the needs of others, and challenges him that just the other day he wanted to be a grand hero. Wilson admits that he has changed. Henry tells him that Jim Conklin is dead. Then Wilson breaks up a potential fight between two light-footed soldiers and a huge bearded man. Known before as a fighter, Wilson has been wholly converted from belligerence to pacifism. He tells Henry that over half the men in the regiment were lost the previous day, but nearly all returned during the night.

NOTES AND GLOSSARY:

charnel place . . . prophecy: the sleeping soldiers seem dead now, but they will be dead by one means or another later; compare Whitman's 'long panoramas of visions' in 'When Lilacs Last in the Dooryard Bloomed'

no more a loud young soldier: in just a day Wilson has changed, the regiment has changed, and Henry has changed

rebs: rebels, or Confederate soldiers

Chapter 15

Standing in formation next to Wilson, Henry hesitates after his first impulse to bring up the subject of the yellow envelope that Wilson gave him on the occasion of the first battle. Henry thinks that he can use the packet as a weapon against his friend whenever he needs to. He feels superior to Wilson because while he himself made his mistakes in the dark, Wilson admitted weakness to him openly. Fleming feels superior not only to Wilson but to circumstances also. In his pride he even thinks he is somehow chosen to be spared in this war. As he ascends to great heights of self-congratulation, Wilson humbly asks for his papers. Fleming is proud not to mock his friend, and he envisions himself as a hero, recounting battles to ladies at home.

NOTES AND GLOSSARY:

yellow envelope: the symbol given by Wilson to Fleming in Chapter 3

black landscape: a scene painted with cynicism about the hopelessness of life; here begins Crane's use of black in many contexts

the chosen of gods: as in Homer's works wherein men are favoured by some gods and hounded by others

Chapter 16

The regiment takes a position marked out by the men it is relieving. The men lie in rifle pits listening to the gunfire; then after it stops they withdraw to re-position. They grumble and talk of the regiment's bad luck. Fleming is particularly critical of the general, but he is brought low by a sarcastic man whose remarks remind him of his shame. In a clear space the men dig in to face the enemy. Fleming continues his savage criticisms until the lieutenant shuts him up. Then the Confederate charge begins as the men woodenly await it.

NOTES AND GLOSSARY:
fracas: disturbance
genie: demon
pot shot: careless shot
chin music: idle talk, like *jawin'* earlier in the chapter

Chapter 17

Fatigued by yesterday's ordeal of flight and return, Henry directs his anger and hatred toward the enemy. His hatred is so concentrated that he loses consciousness of everything else, and only when he hears the laughter of one of his comrades does he realise that the enemy has retreated. His regiment has been observing his fierce fighting with awe. Now the lieutenant uses him as a model of a good soldier, enthusiastically praising his spirit. Fleming thinks he now is a hero as he observes the elation of his fellow soldiers.

NOTES AND GLOSSARY:
a piler men: a pile of men

Chapter 18

Against the sound of battle, Jimmie Rogers, who has been wounded, writhes and calls for help. Wilson and Fleming depart to fill canteens, and on their return observe the front from a hillside. A general and his staff ride up, and to the youths' amazement call the 304th a 'lot 'a mule drivers', who will be sent on an almost impossible mission with heavy casualties expected. Fleming is impressed by the insignificance of his regiment in the general's view. The friends race back to tell their men that they will charge. Indeed the officers soon prepare the charge. The friends have kept the remark about the 'mule drivers' secret.

NOTES AND GLOSSARY:
spanged: slapped

Chapter 19

The charge begins, and Henry is in the front of the mass of moving men. Enemy fire kills many while the regiment seems blind to consequences. After running forward, the regiment stops and slowly considers itself with its ranks thinned by the merciless fire. The lieutenant tries to urge the paralysed men forward, but Henry's cry rouses Wilson to fire and to inspire the men to fight. The advance continues against increasingly heavy fire to the edge of an open space leading to the enemy lines. The lieutenant and Fleming have words about a further advance movement, and then they are joined by Wilson to inspire the men. Around the flag they yell and exhort, then move forward with the regiment, now depleted, behind them. As he charges forward, Henry becomes emotionally bonded to the flag when suddenly the colour-bearer is hit and goes down. Springing forward, Henry and Wilson grab the pole and wrench it away from the dying man.

NOTES AND GLOSSARY:
goddess, radiant: always a symbol, the flag becomes here a living force, beautiful, invulnerable, and commanding

Chapter 20

The men have become dejected and try to retreat as the officers call them back. Henry pushes his friend away from the flag while the regiment takes cover behind some trees. Now enraged that the regiment is proving itself to be a bunch of mule drivers, Henry hates the general who so named them. Yet the situation deteriorates and the fragments of the regiment near Henry seem to be under fire from all directions. After a short time, the enemy charges. Instead of old troops, these Confederate soldiers seem to have new uniforms, and they seem to have been taken by surprise by the lieutenant's men. The volleys of the Union soldiers force a retreat, and soon the field is empty except for the dead. This gives the regiment its confidence back.

NOTES AND GLOSSARY:
illusions: allusions
buffed: (*archaic*) struck

Chapter 21

The men retreat in high spirits to their own lines, where they meet with the usual mockery of soldiers. Henry Fleming is surprised to see how short a distance they covered in their charge and how spent they all seem now. The officer who has called the 304th mule drivers now berates Colonel MacChesnay for not pressing forward for a victory. He calls the men 'mud diggers', and points out the firing that indicates just why the men should have pushed on. The lieutenant voices his dissatisfaction with the general's remarks, but is silenced by the colonel. Wilson and Fleming discuss the situation and agree that they did well when a soldier reports a conversation he has overheard between the colonel and Lieutenant Hasbrouck. The colonel praised both Fleming and Wilson for their valour and the lieutenant also praised them. The two friends are both secretly pleased by this report.

NOTES AND GLOSSARY:

deacon: layman appointed to assist the minister of a Protestant congregation
jimhickey: fine fellow

Chapter 22

Henry Fleming watches the battle with serene detachment. He watches the advances and retreats and hears the guns burst out of the silences. He sees his own regiment gain new strength. When the enemy approaches, the regiment forces it to hide behind a wandering line of fence. The regiment is resolved not to budge. Men drop all around, and though courageous, the men remaining are becoming weak.

NOTES AND GLOSSARY:

gluttering: spluttering (*Oxford English Dictionary*, glutter), or perhaps a misprint for 'glittering'
frowzled: slovenly, dishevelled

Chapter 23

The colonel gives the order to charge. All the men are enthusiastic about this, and they rise with vigour. Against this mad rush of men, the Confederate soldiers cannot stand firm, and they begin to retreat. Henry focuses his attention on the enemy's flag and charges to possess it. The wounded body of the enemy colour-bearer still holds the flag aloft, but Wilson overcomes all obstacles and seizes it. There is great rejoicing over the apparent victory. Prisoners react differently to their captivity. The two friends with their two flags congratulate each other.

NOTES AND GLOSSARY:

for dissections: for thorough analysis
treasure of mythology: like the Golden Fleece of Greek legend or, perhaps, the golden apples of the Hesperides

Chapter 24

When the noises of battle cease, the regiment is ordered to retrace its hard-fought way back across the river. As the regiment moves toward the river, the men are relieved that for now the battle is over. Fleming begins to recount to himself what happened and what part he played in it. Intruding upon his feeling of oneness with a kind nature is the remembrance of the tattered man, whom he betrayed. Gradually Henry is able to detach himself from the haunting image of the tattered man. He plans to use the memory to keep himself humble. He now feels a quiet manhood within himself. His soul has changed and former visions of the nature of heroism have passed away.

NOTES AND GLOSSARY:

stentorian: very loud and far-reaching
swan: (*American slang*) swear

Part 3

Commentary

Nature, purpose and achievement of the work

The Red Badge of Courage stands out not only as one of the major war novels in world literature, but also, from the time of its first publication, as one of the greatest and most popular works in American literature. It is now the single best-known work taught almost everywhere in American schools and colleges because of its clarity of presentation and its powerful message about the effects of experience on a young man's mind. The impact of *The Red Badge of Courage*, not limited just to American literature, extended in its own day to the early British stream-of-consciousness writers and to Crane's acquaintance Joseph Conrad, as well as to countless others worldwide who read the work in translation.

Not as long as a full novel, yet more sweeping in its scope than most novellas, or short novels, *The Red Badge of Courage* at times also seems more like a prose poem, with sensitivity, colour, and even style and rhythm similar to those in Crane's free verse. Ironically, although set in and inextricably bound to the circumstances of the American Civil War, *The Red Badge of Courage* is not very important for documenting particulars of the military history of that war. Instead, *The Red Badge of Courage* shows the evolution of the mind and character of young Henry Fleming, a lowly private soldier. In this respect the novel could be considered a *Bildungsroman*, or a novel of a young man's education; yet from Goethe's *Wilhelm Meister's Apprenticeship* onward, the novel of education generally covered more than just a few days' experiences and progressed gradually through all the stages of development from youth to sober maturity. The use of war as a setting and subject of his novel allowed Crane to compress the almost epic development of his hero Henry Fleming into a very short time. Later James Joyce (1882-1941) was to refine this technique further, compressing an epic exploration of the collective mind of Dublin into a matter of hours in *Ulysses* (1922) and the collective mind of man into a matter of minutes in *Finnegans Wake* (1939).

Constructed in twenty-four chapters to resemble, superficially, the twenty-four book structure of both the *Iliad* and *Odyssey*, the epic poems of Greek antiquity, *The Red Badge of Courage* is also sprinkled (very sparingly) with allusions to the Classical epics. Yet *The Red Badge of Courage* is an epic only in the sense that Henry Fleming's experience itself is epic in scope. The fact that Henry Fleming is a mere private soldier and not the progenitor of his race and people, suggests something about Crane's ideas about the natural nobility of the common man. In fact, the novel's lyrical beauty on the one hand and attention to particular details on the other, suggest a total revision of old epic ideas in favour of surprising new ones. Epic imagery and some aspects of epic form lie buried in the text while new images and symbols emerge and supersede them. *The Red Badge of Courage* was, without apparent effort, unabashedly shaped to be an American epic.

The Red Badge of Courage is Crane's best known work, though he wrote at least two short stories that in their own genre are considerable achievements – particularly 'The Open Boat' and 'The Monster'. Just as he had written *Maggie* before he went to New York City to experience the life he so vividly described, so he wrote *The Red Badge of Courage* with no experience of the American Civil War and became a war correspondent only after that book's publication. Unlike his novel's hero Henry Fleming, Crane had the gift of being able to re-create truth imaginatively, and he seems to have written something essentially true and universal about the condition of man. The book's twin themes of guilt and freedom, courage and cowardice, illusion and reality, doubt and truth, death and life, indicate the range of experience he has surveyed. But overlying the deep questions about experience, nature, and man's place in the universe that lie behind the action is a rich texture of details that lie more or less on the surface. Many of these details are memorable and serve as symbols with profound meaning.

The Red Badge of Courage is full of symbols. Objects, colours, actions and even characters are often symbolical. The creative imagination of Henry Fleming brings these symbols to life. Curiously one of the strengths of the novel proceeds from the resilience and flexibility of Henry's picture-forming mind. Henry tends to see the world through a series of symbols. He apprehends the world imaginatively, constantly seeking for meaning even where there may be none. Also, Crane's dual perspective, at times purely objective and unrelated to a particular mind and at other times still objective but viewed specifically through Henry's mind and eyes, provides the reader with at least two complementary modes of experience. And since Henry's perspective is constantly changing through his growth to maturity, a sense of realism is achieved through different and even contradictory ideas in layers on top of one another in the same mind.

Perhaps the greatest achievement of *The Red Badge of Courage* is its emphasis on war's ability to test and transform men in positive ways. War novels contemporaneous with *The Red Badge of Courage*, such as Émile Zola's *Le Débâcle* and Leo Tolstoy's *Sketches of Sebastopol*, and also the American reviews of such works, influenced Crane, but the other war novels do not have the focus on feelings or the abiding hope that Crane wrote into *The Red Badge of Courage*. Such later war novels as Erich Maria Remarque's (*b*. 1898) *All Quiet on the Western Front* (1929) and Norman Mailer's (*b*. 1923) *The Naked and the Dead* (1948) contrast strikingly with *The Red Badge of Courage* by dwelling on the dehumanising qualities of the war experience. Without diminishing war's mindless brutality, Crane made war a representation of experience, even of life itself, compressed and intense and forcing a deep consideration of values at every point because of the mortal stakes involved. Not war but man is the dominant strain in *The Red Badge of Courage*, and Henry Fleming manages to rise above the circumstances of war without losing his humanity or his credibility.

The Red Badge of Courage stands out from contemporaneous war novels as much by its style as by its treatment of major themes. Zola and Tolstoy cluttered their works with details that merely describe; Crane economised, using only what he needed to evoke a mood or suggest a cluster of meanings. Crane's novel is sparse; its antiquarian interest is almost non-existent. In contrast his reporting of war as a journalist for the New York syndicate is factual and detailed. In his journalism he naturally aimed at a style that would not only capture the interest of his readers but enable them to envisage in concrete terms the situations he was describing. *The Red Badge of Courage*, though printed in newspapers before being published in book form, is very clearly a literary work with no claims to reportage.

The background

The Red Badge of Courage appeared long enough after the Civil War to have a readership either too young to remember the hostilities or too old and tired of the war to recall very clearly minute details. A full generation had grown up since the end of the war, and Americans were eager for war stories because the horror of war had dimmed with time. From another perspective, the United States was far enough from the impact of the war experience to be ready to go to war again. *The Red Badge of Courage* became part of the prelude to the Spanish-American War. It was not propaganda as such, but its effect was to emphasise in the popular imagination the heroic possibilities of war. This was ironical because *The Red Badge of Courage* was not commissioned as propaganda but instead grew out of Crane's need to tell a simple story.

The story fired the imagination of a generation ready for heroism, and one accidental reason for the work's popularity was the timing of its first appearance. Another popular feature of the book was its emphasis on patriotism. *The Red Badge of Courage* is sanctioned as universal reading material in America because although war is often shown to be cruel and irrational in the book, Henry Fleming is loyal and patriotic to the core. He never questions the cause of the war or doubts what the proper action in a war should be. Twentieth-century cynicism about patriotism was not even hinted at in Crane's novel.

For all the novel's appeal to patriotism in provincial America, *The Red Badge of Courage* does not rely for its effects on the depiction of regional character types or on dialect. Later Norman Mailer would use the non-American roots of his characters to distinguish them in *The Naked and the Dead*. In that way Mailer showed just what a melting pot of world cultures America was during the Second World War. But Crane makes no issue of national origins or of the particular states that produced the soldiers. Even the northern and southern soldiers are only vaguely distinguished from each other. In a time when for the first time men of different states fought in the same arena since the American Revolution, the Civil War might have seemed to provide an opportunity for a panorama of the American people. Instead Crane focused on a nondescript provincial farm boy as a representative of boys like him, regardless of their states of origin. The outlook of the novel is thereby more universal because it is not restricted by local colour. Further, the differences in soldiers from the various states would have evoked criticisms of his handling of them, and Crane had larger aims in view.

The United States was ready for *The Red Badge of Courage* to appear first in newspapers not only because of the kind of journalism that was pouring from the presses but also because of the moulding of literary tastes that had occurred since the Civil War. Journalism in the late nineteenth century was more lively and more geared to a good story than it was in the time after the First World War (1914-18). Literacy had made great progress since the early part of the nineteenth century, and the newspaper industry, secure in its position as the major mass medium of its time, had grown to meet a broader and larger audience. Abuses of the medium were widespread, and only after the turn of the twentieth century was the newspaper industry regulated from within with any clear guidelines. Publishers looked for material that would sell, politicians looked to the newspapers for propaganda, and the readers of papers looked to the papers as their main contact with a larger reality than their homes and work. The urbanisation of America, while still in its infancy, provided the press with a readership near at hand in the cities. With the need for copy and with the syndicates being able to buy talent such as that of Stephen Crane, newspapers became a haven for writers whose living depended on their pen. The line between fact and fiction was not clear. Where today magazines, television, photography, and film can serve as a check or balance on newspaper reportage, in Crane's day the weekly and monthly magazines complemented the newspapers, which remained uncontrolled.

The wide influence of the press contributed to popular taste. Since many of the emerging writers wrote for newspapers, they naturally carried over journalistic technique into their literary work. The vogue for realism was in part a result of the influence of the dominant medium and of the press correspondents whose talent was a blend of factual reporting and popular story-telling. It would be a mistake to think of realism as the dominant mode in the literature of this period. American popular literature was sentimental, often trite, and affected. Twain mercilessly satirised American literature and American society throughout his career, and with good reason. The realists were in the minority. Few journalists showed the good judgment of Crane, Twain, and some others. The literary figures whom discerning readers enjoy today were protected and nurtured by William Dean Howells and his friends, who were bent on changing public tastes. But Howells granted his support to writers who rose above the general level of American literature. Only the school of experience might produce the kind of writing he admired and helped to publish.

Crane's move to New York City in the early stages of his career was the result of his being a native of the middle Atlantic region who would naturally move there for experience – New York City was, of course, the literary capital of America. Howells himself moved from Boston to New York and took with him the sensibility which was the dominant force in American literature for thirty years. The New England school of writers, which boasted Emerson and Thoreau and which won such unlikely figures as Melville, was finally eclipsed by the more democratic movement in New York. Despite its position as America's main literary centre, New York proved unsatisfactory to Crane and other 'exile' American writers who moved to London. The best in literature was produced during this period by uprooted men such as Henry James, Joseph Conrad, and Crane himself.

The internationalism of literary figures allowed a rich cross-fertilisation of influences during this period. Literary movements that were Continental or English, such as naturalism and determinism, were assimilated by writers whose own personal visions influenced their interpretations of the movements or drew their often conflicting influences together in new syntheses. Crane was not only aware of international movements; he consciously incorporated their influence in his work. Take for example Henry Fleming, the hero of *The Red Badge of Courage*. He is a remarkably free agent when compared with other heroes of the realistic school of late nineteenth-century American literature. He is not a 'naturalistic' hero because his background does not seem to have much to do with his reactions or development and because the war environment remains largely unaffected by nature. Fleming is certainly not determined or fated to act as he does. He is a free agent. Although images of entrapment or enslavement fill the book, Fleming can make his own decisions, whether running, returning, or standing his ground. He is clearly not a deterministic hero.

An impression of realism arises from Fleming's freedom to choose, and the moral appeal in him is based on the choices he makes. He is not perfect, but he suffers from guilt for what he has not done well. In this respect, and possibly in the way in which he perceives the world as full of symbols, Fleming's mind is in part a reflection of a deep strain of Methodism in Crane's own mind, ingrained early in his life by his father the itinerant Methodist preacher.

The Red Badge of Courage does not offer a probing investigation of the causes of the American Civil War. Henry Fleming is confident that the North will win, but he never asks why the war is being fought at all. His criticisms of the war extend to the generals and no further. They do not extend to the government or to this particular war itself. He brings to the war an idealistic, youthful attitude and many illusions – about war and about his own relation to nature and the great abstractions. As his early illusions are shattered, new ones take shape in his imagination. The circumstances of war and the transformations that take place within him break up his tidy impressions of wholeness in the universe. Any initial or residual Emersonian idealism in the novel is at odds with the realism of a grim meaninglessness and seemingly mindless destruction of human life. Further, the war itself becomes almost a character in the work, and in this respect it is like nature, except that war has the power to destroy where nature merely provides a neutral backdrop for destruction of man by man. Yet Fleming finds refuge in individual heroism, and he seems indestructible, like the flag he carries into the final battle. The novel bears little resemblance to earlier war literature from the Homeric epics and the *Lysistrata* of Aristophanes (*c.*448-*c.*380BC) to Shakespeare's (1564-1616) *Troilus and Cressida* or *Henry V*. Among the earlier attitudes to war the sentiments of the Roman poet Vergil's epic, the *Aeneid*, are perhaps closest to those in *The Red Badge of Courage*.

Classical literature would not have been unknown to Stephen Crane. American education in his time included a healthy dose of both Greek and Latin literature, particularly for a young man who went to college. Like any other schoolboy of his time he would have known stories from the great Greek and Roman epics, the *Iliad*, the *Odyssey*, and the *Aeneid*. Naturally Henry Fleming's mind reflects on Classical models of heroism when he faces the enormities of war. But none of the Classical epics had a hero like Fleming, and none of them was told from so intimate a point of view as Fleming's story. Crane's references to Classical figures, such as the unfortunate Icarus, are subtle, and the casual references to gods as favourable or otherwise, or to the war god as swollen with blood, give more the taste than the substance of Classical works.

Perhaps the most striking aspect of the external background in *The Red Badge of Courage* is how very little of it there is. Very little background knowledge is required of a reader for a full appreciation of the work. This kind of allusion-free writing would have been as appropriate in Crane's day as in our own for the mass medium of the newspaper. He would not have wished to put off his readers or his publisher with any but the most obvious allusions. In addition Crane seems to have had some contempt for the pedantry of Classical scholars in his day with their emphasis on knowledge of all of the minute details in ancient literature, and he seems to have gone out of his way not to burden *The Red Badge of Courage* with arcane or antiquarian details. Yet at the same time, Crane constructed *The Red Badge of Courage* in its broad outlines so as to resemble the old epics directly and unmistakably. Unlike Melville's monumental *Moby Dick*, which achieves its epic stature through amplification, the technique of heaping on details from nearly every available context, *The Red Badge of Courage* achieves its unity and integrity, even its epic scope, through omission of all but the barest essentials. From the textual evidence it is clear that even after Crane reworked his short manuscript into a longer one, he then went back to delete whole passages before its publication. The novel gives few names, places, commands, pieces of military equipment, or allusions to other works of literature, yet how large, even expansive the work is for all that!

Stephen Crane's writing has been compared to the technique of the French impressionist painters. Literary impressionism is difficult to define since the painters defined their movement by the effect of light on pools of colour and not by the effect of words. Joseph Conrad, who knew Stephen Crane, called his style 'impressionistic', and he might have had *The Red Badge of Courage* in mind when he criticised Crane for the superficiality of his literary impressionism. In Crane's work colours flash by, scenes emerge and recede as if in a fog, and Henry Fleming's volatile mind turns from idea to image to new idea repeatedly. Few details seem to be drawn incisively or clearly except for such powerful and haunting images as the 'red wafer' or the 'black ants swarming greedily upon the gray face', or such powerful actions as Fleming's flight, Conklin's death, the tattered man, the wounding of Fleming, Wilson's tenderness, the young friends' final triumph. The best effects of *The Red Badge of Courage* are not to be found on the work's surface, which is difficult to define precisely, but in the succession of emotions that are evoked in the reader. Crane's purpose was to create a war novel that would at one and the same time capture the feeling of going through an experience of cosmic dimensions and transmit that feeling with no intermediary or extraneous details.

The political, economic, and social dimensions of *The Red Badge of Courage* are almost non-existent. Although the end of the nineteenth century brought sweeping changes in America, these developments are not even alluded to in the novel. As for the political, social, and geographical aspects of America in the period of the Civil War, Crane is not concerned with them. Instead, philosophical and vaguely religious ideas emerge from *The Red Badge of Courage*. Crane deals more in abstract values such as courage and charity than in Populism or *laissez faire*. Where in *Maggie* social problems are explicitly examined, in *The Red Badge of Courage* Crane leaves present reality behind. War seems to wipe out all considerations except the basic instinct for survival. Even the technological aspects of warfare are not allowed to get in the way of Crane's purpose. Machine metaphors are used throughout, but they are not very specific. The war could not easily be confused with other wars because of certain details, but it is meant to be a universal theatre of war, not a local, time-bound one.

Crane wrote *The Red Badge of Courage* after one of the most severe economic recessions of the century involving a failure of confidence in the banking system. Because of his own struggle to make his way in dire times, the economic motive behind his writing was urgent. Yet Crane struggled for quality, rewriting his work repeatedly. Only when his debts in England were beyond bearing did his art suffer. *The Red Badge of Courage* came out before he was famous and before he had personal obligations. Living at subsistence level and fighting daily for survival, Crane was ideally suited to sympathise with Henry Fleming's mind. For five years Crane eked out a living by writing for newspapers, and even after the acclaim of *Maggie* he had to scrape together a living. He had, in short, first-hand experience of Darwinian selection. He survived for the time. Ironically, even after *The Red Badge of Courage* appeared and his big chance came as a war correspondent, Crane did not achieve wealth and spent his time writing furiously to meet his mounting obligations.

Structure

Henry Fleming's story is for the most part a self-contained narrative. Occasionally Henry thinks about his home and mother, as in Chapter 1, or about details of village life, as when he pictures the circus parade or imagines his mother and the young girl from the seminary listening to his glorious tales of personal heroism, but usually Henry remembers only those details and scenes that the reader has experienced with him. We do not discover very much about Fleming's past before the war. The overall pattern of flight, return, and triumph, is consequently extremely simple, but it gains in complexity with the careful elaboration of the changes in Henry's outlook.

The twenty-four chapters of *The Red Badge of Courage* bear a superficial resemblance to the twenty-four book structure of both the *Odyssey* and the *Iliad*. But a more significant reason for this particular number of chapters is the property of the number twenty-four to be divided in different ways. Crane seems to have used this property to help to unify his work. For example, the first half of the book (Chapters 1 to 12) concerns Henry's flight from battle and return to his regiment. The second half (Chapters 13 to 24) concerns Henry's growing friendship with Wilson and his evolving heroism.

The overall balance between the two halves of the book is enhanced by a subtle relationship of smaller segments within each half. The first quarter of the book (Chapters 1 to 6) is parallel in structure to the third quarter (Chapters 13 to 18). As an example of one pair of details, in Chapter 3 Wilson gives Fleming his yellow envelope, but in Chapter 15 (which is parallel to Chapter 3) Wilson retrieves it. Mechanical battles occur in the paired Chapters 5 and 17. Likewise, the second quarter of the book (Chapters 7 to 12) is parallel in structure to the fourth quarter (Chapters 19 to 24). For example, in Chapter 11 Fleming has the irresistible desire to return to the war, and in the parallel Chapter 23 he is driven to triumph irresistibly. The chapters of the book therefore contain elements that unify and clarify the progress of Henry's maturation.

The intricacy of Crane's structure extends to colour patterns, key memories, and characters, and it is enough to say that if the reader begins to examine *The Red Badge of Courage* for underlying elements that tend to unify the work, he will find them. Crane did not intend his structural elements to be obtrusive. On the contrary, he was careful to make his parallels as subtle as possible. The evidence of his many revisions of the book indicates an unusual care with craftsmanship. Rather than flowing from his pen unconsciously, *The Red Badge of Courage* is a deliberately planned and created complete work.

More important, however, than a consideration of the mechanics of the book's structure is the impression created by reading the work that something whole and universal has been unveiled. This impression arises from a plausible development in Fleming's attitudes and perceptions. The consistency of Henry's youthful mind through all its changes, and his ability to adapt to and even to master experiences as the story progresses, provide the strongest unifying element. Supporting Henry's development and giving it breadth and depth is the relation of the actions of other characters to his own. Clearly Wilson and Fleming have both developed along parallel lines. The development of Hasbrouck, the lieutenant, is in many respects like the development of Henry. In an even larger perspective, the entire regiment develops much like Henry, who represents its spirit at nearly every point. Henry is representative not only of what happens to one man in battle, but what happens to men in groups in battle. For all his differences from his comrades, Henry's mind is the collective consciousness of the Union Army. Consider, for example, the news that not just Henry but nearly the entire regiment somehow was thought to have perished in the first encounter; during the night the other men, like Henry, wander back. The reader is not told the story of each returning soldier, but Crane implies that at least some of the other men may have undergone similar fears and even taken to flight like Henry. Henry is singled out by his wound, as well as by his ability to turn a personal defeat into a final, decisive victory.

Style

The word 'impressionism' is often used to describe the style of *The Red Badge of Courage*. The French impressionist painters, such as Claude Monet and Pierre Auguste Renoir (1841-1919), painted in different individual styles, but all of them had in common an interest in the effects of light and colour. Their paintings are not about sharp outlines, but about the way in which pools of light relate to each other to produce an image. Often the subject of an impressionist painting is only identifiable from a distance; close to the image dissolves into a myriad of brush strokes in brilliant colour. At least one impressionist painter used long-handled brushes to that he could stand back far enough from his canvases to do them justice. In general, impressionist painters concentrated on landscapes, still-lifes, portraiture, architecture, city scenes, and interior scenes rather than on historical, documentary or anatomical subjects. But even so, impressionists had a dual interest – in surface effects of light and in the quality of the world around them. A mistake in criticism of works in this style is to take the surface for the whole work.

Crane used colours like the impressionist painters, but naturally, working in a different medium, he used the full range of literary expression also. The title *The Red Badge of Courage* signals the symbolic use of one of the dominant colours in the book. Red is used directly in the novel or obliquely in references to human bloodshed. In the last quarter of the book the colour black is used increasingly. A variety of colours is to be found in nearly every chapter. Although some colours are used to make the narrative come to life, others have more than merely a surface meaning. These are discussed below in the section on 'Theme and symbol'. Crane's use of colours is complemented by his use of the smoke of the battlefield, the fog and haze produced by the weather, and the sunlight, firelight, and darkness of the night. Like images in impressionist paintings, Crane's images often seem more like flashes or patches of colour emerging from a murky background than clearly identifiable, hard-edged forms. The book's visual images are related to the slow, unsure process of formation of ideas in Henry's mind. Clearly Crane's emphasis on colour goes beyond that of most of the authors who were his contemporaries. And his repeated use of the same colours gives a sense of unity and, by their accumulation, of power to his novel.

Crane's style is also distinguished by its lack of specific reference, lack of dialectal differences in his characters' speech, lack of allusions to other works of literature and art, and lack of detailed characterisation, except in Henry, the central figure. The absence of all these can be related to Crane's impressionism and also to the quality of mind of Henry Fleming, who is by and large an average youth with an active imagination. Fleming's sensibility includes a tendency to philosophise on or rationalise all experience and a tendency to think of events on the battlefield in terms of his village background (domestic images) and village schooling (a taste for Classical virtues). For example, a regiment preparing to repel an attack is compared to a group of ladies trying on new hats, and war is at first a glorious epic adventure.

Because Crane wrote in the third person singular, it is difficult to tell when the reader is inside Henry's mind and when he is outside it. This ambiguity in point of view is useful in letting the reader experience the descriptive passages for himself. When Henry is trying to come to grips with himself or his guilt or his elation, the reader is sufficiently detached by the third-person narration to view those attempts objectively, sometimes even clinically. But when aspects of nature become major symbols, it is not often clear that they are seen as such by Henry himself – as with the famous image of the sun as a red wafer. Within these limits, Crane is consistent throughout. Arising from these limits is another feature of Crane's style – his use of symbols. The novel is replete with symbols, and it is often difficult to tell where symbolism leaves off and pure description begins.

Theme and symbol

Crane goes beyond simple impressionism in the sweep of the themes and the profundity of the symbols in *The Red Badge of Courage*. A theme is a word, like *death* or *war* or *nature*, that takes on significance as a major element, stressed in a literary work. A symbol is a thing, person, animal, image or action, that seems to be charged with meaning – a flag or a dead man may be a symbol. *The Red Badge of Courage* deals with many themes and contains numerous symbols. It gains its power from the way the themes and symbols inter-relate.

Crucial themes in *The Red Badge of Courage* are found in opposition to each other. For example, cowardice is opposed to courage and guilt is opposed to remorse. The conflict in these opposites seems even more important than the conflict between the two armies, which wore the blue and grey uniforms respectively. Henry's feelings oscillate between hostility and friendship, shame and bravado, foolishness and profundity, flight and triumph, lies and sincere truthfulness. Crane's use of yoked but antagonistic or antithetical themes is both subtle and complex. For example, cowardice and courage are usually thought of as opposites; yet Crane has shown in *Red Badge* how cowardice can lead to courage, just as in the character of Wilson combativeness yields to humility. Crane then shows the relationships between opposite themes, and the way in which war can ironically transform one theme into its opposite. For example, Henry awakens in the morning after he has returned to his regiment and at first thinks that all the other sleeping men around him are dead; then he knows that they are alive; then he realises that some day they all will be dead as they at first glance seem to be. Such shifting perspectives, with their ironies of contradiction, enrich and deepen a simple life-against-death opposition. The living and the dead are intimately related and Fleming gains in maturity from understanding something about this relationship.

Symbols are not easily explained in *The Red Badge of Courage*, but seem to contain more meaning than can be described in a few sentences. Perhaps the most significant symbol for Henry is the dressing for his head wound. The dressing is a badge (or symbol) of courage, but actually it was not earned in battle at all. In fact, it was a mistake – a blow dealt by a man who was himself fleeing. Yet the badge allows Henry to develop as a hero; it gives him status and dignity. More than that, it is a sign of Wilson's friendship. Wilson dressed the wound with his own handkerchief. So it is a badge of cowardice-turned-into heroism and alienation-turned-into-charity. It is also like the lieutenant's hand wound, with the difference that the latter is clearly a genuine badge of courage, earned on the field of battle and subconsciously used as a sign of Hasbrouck's heroism in the final battle.

Another symbol in *The Red Badge of Courage* is the flag, which Henry takes over and carries to lead the charges that give his regiment victory. It is a symbol of the Union and a symbol of unity for the regiment. But it is also a personal symbol for Henry. It almost comes to life for him as a goddess, radiant, immortal in its inspiration. Henry and Wilson grapple for the Union flag, but Henry pushes his friend aside to gain possession of it. Later Wilson obtains a parallel symbol from the dying rebel colour-bearer – the Confederate flag. The two friendly rivals carry their flags into battle together, thus underscoring the parallel between Henry and Wilson right to the end of the book and suggesting the larger unity between North and South that will emerge from the conflict.

On the one hand there are complex symbols like the red badge or the flag; on the other simple, flat symbols like the squirrel that runs from Henry in the forest. Then there are almost awesome symbols that defy interpretation, yet hold mystery upon mystery, such as the sun as a red wafer. Part of the natural symbolism (which includes the squirrel, the forest, the sky, and the sun in other contexts than the one just mentioned), this powerful symbol also draws upon the symbolism of the colour red as brought out elsewhere in the book, but then in addition it contains an allusion to the mystery of the sacrament of Christian Communion, defying analysis and standing for the sacrament most intimately incorporating the divine in the human.

Character also operates on the symbolic level in *The Red Badge of Courage*. Jim Conklin has been seen by some critics as a sacrificial figure. As such his suffering is like that of Jesus Christ, whose initials he shares. The tattered man becomes, by this same line of thought, a symbol of betrayal and uncharitableness for Henry because Henry turned his back on the man. Wilson evolves from a symbol of natural belligerence to a symbol of humility and charity and friendship. The man with the cheery voice is almost a symbol of Henry's guardian angel. Henry Fleming, in addition to drawing together all themes, is a representative of all of them too. From the fat soldier, who tries to steal the horse, to Fleming himself, a full range of symbolic characters is portrayed. Characterisation does not matter beyond the point of making a character plausible; after that symbolic functions in the novel seem to have an equal role with naturalistic ones. *The Red Badge of Courage* comes close in some respects to the medieval morality plays, and, like *Everyman* (*c.* 1500), asks for a universal understanding.

Both theme and symbol involve irony, for opposite meanings can exist together in the same symbol just as opposite themes can derive strength from each other. Since themes and symbols are repeated with slight (often more than slight) variations throughout the book, they serve also to unify the book and give it depth.

Part 4

Hints for study

READING IS AN ART. It takes time, patience, and careful attention. Most people – even some so-called professionals – read too rapidly and with only a fraction of the attention that is needed. They read in fits and starts. They stop in the middle of an action and turn immediately to some other task. They do not pause to reflect while they read. They resist the temptation to look back to an earlier passage when the text seems to suggest that they do so. If you are going to avoid their mistakes, take the time to consider how you read and how you can read best. Then arrange a time and a place for reading and reflection. Use good lighting, have a sharp pencil handy, and trust your own good judgment. If a book is worth reading, it is worth reading well. Read well, a book will remain part of you, and you will remember it accurately and with pleasure.

You need to trust not only yourself when you read but your author as well. An outstanding author has an individual style, wholly unlike that of any other writer. His work will give you clues as to how to understand it. Your accurate interpretation will depend on how well you follow the directions the author provides for you. Often you will discover ideas in a book that no other reader seems to have found. This is not necessarily a sign that your reading is bad. In fact, you may be reading the work better than anyone else ever has. After all, your experience, being unique, will provide automatically a new perspective on the work. At the same time, beware of an outlandish interpretation that is based on the reading of only one paragraph or chapter.

When you have prepared yourself to read the book, read *The Red Badge of Courage* through without referring to criticisms or even discussions with your friends. Then, while the book is still fresh in your mind, write down your impressions of it in the form of sketches. If certain passages seem in retrospect to be outstanding for the light they shed on major themes in the work, seek them out and copy them word for word with a page reference for each. Try to summarise the action for yourself, and divide your summary into sections and even scenes. In *The Red Badge of Courage* Henry Fleming makes a number of vital decisions. Where decisions are made by Henry or where he seems to change his attitude, define precisely what led up to the decision or change. For example, Henry does not decide to return to his regiment immediately after Jim Conklin dies. First he must come to grips with the reality of death and then he must want to see the battle with its grim work of killing people. Only after that does he decide to return to his regiment. Now locate the major turning-points for Henry without which his story would not take place. At least one such turning-point takes place before the action as we witness it – Henry's decision to enlist, with all it says about the way he makes his crucial decisions.

With your notes to help you, you are now ready for a *second* reading, this time chapter by chapter, with these Notes and a dictionary. Two readings, *at least*, are essential if you are to discuss this work intelligently. During the second and subsequent readings you should consider the sections below, which offer guidance on various aspects of your study, in addition to any ideas you yourself have found interesting.

Most of the dialect in the book can be understood with a little effort. Any words or phrases that stand out as particularly difficult will be found in the 'Notes and glossary' sections of the Notes. You will not need to puzzle through many allusions or search down many hard words. Crane wrote for a mass audience, so his style is easily understood. Do not make the mistake of thinking the novel simplistic on account of this ease of reading. Keep your pace of reading slow enough to pick up points that might otherwise slip past you.

Characters

Little in the way of characterisation occurs in *The Red Badge of Courage* apart from that of Henry Fleming, and this is due in part to the novel's point of view, and in part to the background of battle action. Yet the work is full of characters and they all contribute to the impression of realism in the book.

Make a complete list of the characters in the novel, even if they are only introduced as, for example, 'the fat soldier'. When you can attach a name to a label, as for example, the name Wilson to 'the loud soldier', do so. Try to establish precisely to which chapter(s) each character belongs. Do you notice any patterns emerging? Can you tell which characters are included for more than just 'local colour'? Consider the function of the tattered man or the man with the cheery voice, and compare them with the functions of the fat soldier or the officer with the red beard.

Why is there so little characterisation in the novel? Is this a fault? Relate the way Henry feels about Jim to the way he feels about Wilson or the tattered man. Is there a reason – an artistic reason – for the timely appearance of the tattered man? How many figures emerge from Henry's recollection of his village life? What do you learn about

American village life from the characters presented? How does Henry feel about authority and characters who represent authority? Does his attitude change? Do not forget such diverse persons as the generals and Henry's own mother.

Because more characters remain nameless than are named in the novel, the book seems to operate on one level like a morality play. Characters seem to be present for the moral values they represent. Can you develop this idea with specific reference to the universality of Crane's message? Would you agree with the critics who maintain that Jim Conklin represents Jesus Christ? On what grounds would you agree or disagree?

Structure

The Red Badge of Courage is carefully constructed, not only in terms of its twenty-four chapters but also within each chapter. Draw a line down the centre of a sheet of paper. Then place on the left side of the line the numbers one to twelve. Parallel to these on the right side of the line place the numbers thirteen to twenty-four, leaving enough room for one sentence after each. Then in just one sentence, sum up the action of each chapter. Draw parallels anywhere you can between the actions shown.

Using the same arrangement on a different sheet of paper, draw up an inventory of colours by chapter, or images of dead or dying men, or uses of nature for purposes other than strictly descriptive. Can you relate any structural elements here to the patterns that emerged in the action summaries?

Select the four chapters that you consider form the very centre of the novel's meaning. Break each down into its smallest units. For example, Chapter 1 would have an 'envelope' structure. It opens with the arguments about rumoured engagements with the enemy, then shifts to Henry's recalling what led up to his present predicament, and finally closes with a continuation of the argument. Henry's remembrance of leaving the village may also be broken down into its parts, and so forth. Each chapter has its own structure, but compare the similarities between Chapters 1 and 24. Which other chapters resemble each other in structure?

Crane was a master craftsman. His short stories are among the best in American literature. He shaped the chapters of *The Red Badge of Courage* as twenty-four chapters but also as twenty-four independent units. What does the design of *The Red Badge of Courage* suggest about the design of human experience or of the universe?

Theme and symbol

Make a list of the symbols that you consider most relevant for the central themes in *The Red Badge of Courage*. One clear example is that of the images of dead and dying men. These relate directly to the theme of death and usually involve other themes. In the case of Jim Conklin the themes of suffering and friendship come to mind. A useful means of drawing together themes that may relate to a powerful symbol is to place the symbol in the centre of an otherwise blank page and then to write themes that come to mind all around the symbol. Then underline those themes that are most apt and consider how they relate to each other. Are they complementary or are they antithetical? Finally you can consider the symbol as a whole.

Not every image or idea in a literary work is a symbol. Can you find objects or actions in the novel that seem not to be symbolical at all? Compare these to those that obviously are. You will notice that symbolical elements are presented with some power so that they stand out from their context. Sometimes symbols are presented as part of some other figure of speech, such as a metaphor or a simile, which state or imply a relationship between seemingly unrelated things.

As you explore symbols and themes, you will find that some have a local relevance, their meaning limited to one isolated passage in the novel. Others seem to reflect symbols or themes elsewhere or even are continuously presented in the work. War is not only a setting, but a theme, and since it is an analogue for life itself it is also symbolical. List on a separate sheet themes and symbols that seem to be repeated throughout the novel. Do you see relationships emerging? Consider the Red Badge of Courage itself. You may rank the symbol as one of the most important, yet you may see a theme such as war, growth, or charity as more important than courage. Is it possible that one or more of these themes also adheres to the symbol of the Red Badge?

A symbol may be seen as a cluster of themes with power over memory because of the context provided. Not only you as a reader, but the characters in the novel also see the world's symbolical dimensions. What symbols have the most meaning for Henry? for Jim Conklin? for Wilson? for the tattered man? Do any of these coincide with the symbols you ranked as having particularly significant meaning or meanings? State why or why not.

Often readers overlook obvious symbols because they are limited to one sense or one set of objects. Colour symbolism, for example, is fairly evident in *The Red Badge of Courage*, even in the title. But what about noise? vegetation? animals? machines? And consider silence, fog, and smoke. Can you add other categories? One astute critic of the book saw in the ground itself a symbol. Very often your symbolic imagination will produce an emphasis that is unique because you are who you are. The argument for an element having symbolical overtones is up to you. To read only for symbols can limit your enjoyment of other aspects of a literary work, but to miss the symbolical dimensions of *The Red Badge of Courage* when even the title suggests that you consider them would limit your appreciation of this work.

Conflict and irony

Henry Fleming is driven by conflict. From the war on the outside to ideas clashing inside his mind, Henry is meant not only to arbitrate between irreconcilable forces but also to survive and grow through combat experiences that defy his fertile imagination. Conflict in *The Red Badge of Courage* involves characters, ideas, and even symbols. Conflict often involves irony – while fighting against death the tattered man, for example, claims that he cannot die because a 'swad' of children depend on him. Ironically, he begins to act like the dying Conklin just when the youth Fleming abandons him because he has once again asked about Fleming's non-existent wound. Ironically, too, the memory of betraying the tattered man in his moment of need becomes a constant force of self-reproach for Fleming. But Fleming's resolutions of the conflicts that occur within him, though not very satisfying, ring true because they make him human. What conflicts does Henry resolve? Why might they not be very satisfying? Recall that even the conflicts in the war do not reach satisfactory conclusions. For example, even after the triumphant battle, the regiment withdraws from the ground it has sacrificed so many to take. Life and war agree in their untidiness.

Irony is by its nature involved with conflict. Irony involves paradox and surprise. It is ironical that Henry's cowardice should lead to his courage. It is ironical that war, which seems to reduce human life to meaningless slaughter, is the context within which life's meaning can be found. Can you suggest other instances of irony in the book? Consider not only ironies of situation, but those of character, action, and ideas too. Fleming often fools himself by rationalising his own actions, but he becomes trapped by circumstances or by the waves of guilt in his own mind.

Crane was a deft ironist. Perhaps next to symbols, irony is his greatest literary tool. In this he is influenced by ancient Greek drama. He does not stop to consider ironies for you. Your sensitivity must come into play to winnow out the subtleties. Some examples of irony of situation are as follows: the war propaganda paints war as exciting and heroic, but camp life is boring and frustrating and conflict a terrifying and dehumanising experience; Fleming is wounded by a man who himself is fleeing from battle; Jim Conklin is afraid of being run over by wagons and flees into a field to escape one but dies there. Irony of character can be seen in the following: Wilson is combative at first but becomes the most caring person in the novel; the tattered man's insistence on knowing about Fleming's wound drives Fleming away in his hour of need.

Quotations for illustration

You will want to select from the novel certain quotations which you feel explain aspects of the work. The following are examples of quotations you might select to illustrate the aspects indicated.

Henry Fleming's picture-making mind

In Chapter 14 Henry awakens after his first night back with his regiment and he mistakenly thinks he has been placed in a charnel house, then realises his error:

> About him were the rows and groups of men that he had dimly seen the previous night. They were getting a last draught of sleep before the awakening. The gaunt, careworn features and dusty figures were made plain by this quaint light at the dawning, but it dressed the skin of the men in corpselike hues and made the tangled limbs appear pulseless and dead. The youth started up with a little cry when his eyes first swept over this motionless mass of men, thick-spread upon the ground, pallid, and in strange postures. His disordered mind interpreted the hall of the forest as a charnel place. He believed for an instant that he was in the house of the dead, and he did not dare to move lest these corpses start up, squalling and squawking. In a second, however, he achieved his proper mind. He swore a complicated oath at himself. He saw that this somber picture was not a fact of the present, but a mere prophecy.

Notice how at such moments of visionary intensity, Crane employs alliteration (as in motionless mass of men) and allows nature to conspire with Henry's mind in forming the impression of corpses ('made plain by this quaint light at the dawning'). Crane has first clarified that the men seen are the same that Henry saw the night before. Then as he uses language similar to the previous description of the men in Chapter 13, Henry reacts emotionally to the *appearance* – his 'disordered mind interpreted' the scene as a 'charnel place'. Henry's interpretation becomes a belief, emphasised by fear that these dead will rise and menace him. But then he sees things as they are. Then, just as he condemns himself for his credulity, he makes a further and better interpretation. He sees that his vision of dead men is a prophecy that all these men, and indeed all men everywhere, will be dead. Again alliteration is used to underscore the importance of the realisation (picture . . . present . . . prophecy). As in a poem the perspective here shifts radically from line to line. Crane's imagery at such times is full of energy. Henry's active mind and sensitive feelings receive and transmit the impression with high intensity to the reader. No further comment is made on this striking scene. The mundane description of breaking camp is in a different vein, yet the impact of Henry's profound realisation of man's mortality remains. Unable to come to grips with death earlier in the forest chapel, Henry can now face death calmly.

Symbols

In Chapter 19 Henry Fleming fights alongside the flag that he is to bear through his final triumph. In the following passage, just before the flag becomes his, it takes on life for him and even woos him.

> Within him, as he hurled himself forward, was born a love, a despairing fondness for this flag which was near him. It was a creation of beauty and invulnerability. It was a goddess, radiant, that bended its form with an imperious gesture to him. It was a woman, red and white, hating and loving, that called him with the voice of his hopes. Because no harm could come to it he endowed it with power. He kept near, as if it could be a saver of lives, and an imploring cry went from his mind.

Immediately then the colour-bearer goes down, and Henry clutches at the flag pole. But before this act, the flag has been personified, and before that, deified. It first is loved. Henry's imagination then envisions it as a goddess commanding him. Then it is a woman of romance calling sweetly to him. Now Henry invests the flag with power, and finally an unspecified cry goes out from his mind, the answer to which seems to be the fall of the colour-bearer. Earlier in the book the flag has accumulated meanings, but here they are focused sharply so that Henry and the flag seem linked by destiny. It seems very appropriate, then, that Henry and not his rival Wilson should keep this flag.

A strong argument could be made that the flag here becomes at least as important as the wound dressing (the 'red badge of courage') in the symbolic framework of the novel. And the inherent symbolism of the American flag with its red stripes for the blood of human sacrifice streaming over the white field, casts a new light on the relation of Henry's history to his country's.

Where the flag becomes a symbol in the heat of battle, one dead body becomes a symbol in nature's calm, far from the sounds of battle. Chapter 7 records Henry's farthest flight from the war and his own deepest shame. There, having wandered far into the forest, he seeks the most secret place of refuge, but instead of peace and rest, he finds death. It is a grim sight, in a way a double for himself.

> At length he reached a place where the high, arching boughs made a chapel. He softly pushed the green doors aside and entered. Pine needles were a gentle brown carpet. There was a religious half light. Near the threshold he stopped, horror-stricken at the sight of a thing.
>
> He was being looked at by a dead man who was seated with his back against a columnlike tree. The corpse was dressed in a uniform that once had been blue, but was now faded to a melancholy shade of green. The eyes, staring at the youth, had changed to the dull hue to be seen on the side of a dead fish. The mouth was open. Its red had changed to an appalling yellow. Over the gray skin of the face ran little ants. One was trundling some sort of a bundle along the upper lip.

In shaping this symbol, Crane has used many colours – green, brown, blue, red, yellow, and grey. The natural setting has religious overtones. It is a 'chapel' with 'religious half light'. The 'thing' is not only dead but decaying horribly – the faded Union Army uniform, the dead-fish eyes, the colours of the face and mouth. Ants crawl greedily over the dead face. This vision creates awe in Henry Fleming, and terror drives him back out of the forest ultimately to his regiment and the war. If anything, the memory of the body is even more powerful for him than the actual experience itself:

> He was pursued by the sight of the black ants swarming greedily upon the gray face and venturing horribly near to the eyes.

This experience and its haunting memory are not hallucinations. Fleming actually saw the dead man and recorded in horror the small details that dehumanised the corpse. The natural setting, which seemed to be most inviting and actually was described in religious terms, becomes a green charnel house like the one in Henry's later morning vision. But this image is real. Further, the dead man, like Henry, had sought refuge and found death. The relation between Henry and the dead man is clear. Part of Crane's strategy is to make the equation broader, bringing the reader to an identification through surprise and through graphic, unforgettable details. The reader, like Henry, is trapped by the vision of mortality.

Notice that the symbols of the flag and the dead man are linked through the themes of death and immortality. The flag promises invulnerability; it is the psychic antidote to the image of the dead man, who died outside the heroic limits of the battlefield.

Henry Fleming and Wilson

The bond between these two soldiers is signalled by Wilson's giving Henry 'a little packet done up in a yellow envelope' before the first battle (Chapter 3). The power of this symbol in their complex relationship is brought out in Chapter 15.

> The friend had, in a weak hour, spoken with sobs of his own death. He had delivered a melancholy oration previous to his funeral, and had doubtless in the packet of letters, presented various keepsakes to relatives. But he had not died, and thus he had delivered himself into the hands of the youth.
>
> The latter felt immensely superior to his friend, but he inclined to condescension. He adopted toward him an air of patronizing good humor.
>
> His self-pride was now entirely restored . . . . He had performed his mistakes in the dark, so he was still a man.

The sense of power and pride given to Henry by the possession of the symbol of his friend's fear collapses when Wilson retrieves the packet a few minutes later. Pride of possession turns into pride of generosity as Henry returns the symbol.

Clearly the packet is a symbol not only for the reader but for Henry and Wilson also. And it is a developing, not a static symbol. For Wilson at first it is a symbol of his last effects, the remains that will be his last message to the world. Then when he does not die, the packet is a symbol of his folly and even cowardice. Henry receives the packet as a friend, but later pridefully holds the packet as a symbol of his own superiority over his friend. The return of the packet is also symbolical because Henry now sees it as a sign of his own charity. For the reader the packet is not only a cipher by which the two friends' relationship can be read, but it is also a symbol of the futility of a legacy in a world of everpresent death. It is also a symbol of communication between men, a secret message, never revealed in itself but revealing those who would send it.

Henry Fleming and Lieutenant Hasbrouck

The lieutenant earns the respect of his men, and motivates them through Henry Fleming in the triumphant battle in the second half of the book. While in the first half of the book he is noticed more for his rage in beating back deserters to their posts and for his wounded hand (Chapter 4), later he gains the reputation for being fearless. He does not seem to remember Henry's earlier flight (Chapter 6) after Henry's return. The two become a team in Chapter 19.

> The youth stretched forth his arm. 'Cross there?' His mouth was puckered in doubt and awe.
> 'Certainly. Jest 'cross th' lot! We can't stay here,' screamed the lieutenant. He poked his face close to the youth and waved his bandaged hand. 'Come on!' Presently he grappled with him as if for a wrestling bout. It was as if he planned to drag the youth by the ear on to the assault.
> The private felt a sudden unspeakable indignation against his officer. He wrenched fiercely and shook him off.
> 'Come on yerself, then,' he yelled. There was a bitter challenge in his voice.
> They galloped together down the regimental front. The friend scrambled after them.

The chain reaction – Hasbrouck, Henry, Wilson, the men – creates the charge. The lieutenant waves his symbolic bandaged hand, but finally has to wrestle with Henry before the latter's pride is awakened. Then Henry proceeds as if he were the actual commander – and the men follow. Hasbrouck is a good officer because he knows the combination of inducements and threats necessary to get his men to fight and to feel as if the pride of accomplishment belonged to them.

Hasbrouck and Fleming are really doubles, each reflecting the other even to their respective wounds, and it is appropriate that they should together bring about the victory. Notice that Fleming and Wilson have a similar relationship. Crane has portrayed the human chain necessary to successful warfare.

Henry Fleming and Jim Conklin

Jim Conklin is so powerful a figure that Henry's growth can only continue after his death. He is the figure of stability in Henry's mind. Henry relies on him, and when Henry finds him wounded in Chapter 9, Conklin relies on him.

> But the tall soldier continued to beg in a lowly way. He now hung babelike to the youth's arm. His eyes rolled in the wildness of his terror. 'I was allus a good friend t' yeh, wa'n't I, Henry? I've allus been a pretty good feller, ain't I? An' it ain't much t' ask, is it? Jest t' pull me along outer th' road? I'd do it fer you wouldn't I, Henry?'
> He paused in piteous anxiety to await his friend's reply.

The youth had reached an anguish where the sobs scorched him. He strove to express his loyalty, but he could only make fantastic gestures.

Henry in fact does pull Jim out of the road, but only after the tattered man has told him that a battery is approaching and that he should take Jim aside. The reversal of roles of dependency and Jim's delirious concentration on the threat of the batteries add to the helpless and repetitive pleading in Jim's voice. His death, in some ways noble, is really an unconscious battle for freedom and dignity in the face of an inexorable and hideous mechanical failure of the organism.

He was invaded by a creeping strangeness that slowly enveloped him. For a moment the tremor of his legs caused him to dance a sort of hideous hornpipe. His arms beat wildly about his head in expression of implike enthusiasm.

The dance is, of course, the dance of death. Jim joins the dead man in the forest and a host of other figures in Henry's experience who give him a taste of mortality.

This pillar of strength, even a father figure for the fatherless Henry, changes roles with his youthful friend and becomes 'babelike' in his dependency on him. Henry is not up to the role reversal, though he would like to be. Both of the figures are helpless under the circumstances. Henry cannot do much for Jim, and Jim cannot do much for himself. Even though Jim is spared the crushing death he fears, he cannot escape death absolutely.

Henry Fleming and the tattered man

Even stronger than Jim Conklin's death in Henry's imagination is the questioning of the tattered man, who comes close to being an external version of Henry's own conscience. He is never named, and Henry's betrayal of him will linger in Henry's memory to the end of the book. Finally Henry decides to use the memory of what the tattered man represents as a means of achieving humility in himself.

The following passage from Chapter 10 shows how this man affects Henry.

The simple questions of the tattered man had been knife thrusts to him. They asserted a society that probes pitilessly at secrets until all is apparent. His late companion's chance persistency made him feel that he could not keep his crime concealed in his bosom. It was sure to be brought plain by one of those arrows which cloud the air and are constantly pricking, discovering, proclaiming those things which are willed to be forever hidden. He admitted that he could not defend himself against this agency. It was not within the power of vigilance.

The tattered man has become for Henry a symbol of the public American mind, with its tendency to probe to discover every secret, no matter how desperately held. The power of persistency, and the seeming inevitability that Henry's secret will come out are tempered later in Chapter 24.

For a time this pursuing recollection of the tattered man took all elation from the youth's veins. He saw his vivid error, and he was afraid that it would stand before him all his life. He took no share in the chatter of his comrades, nor did he look at them or know them, save when he felt sudden suspicion that they were seeing his thoughts and scrutinizing each detail of the scene with the tattered soldier.

Yet gradually he mustered force to put the sin at a distance.

The tattered man has in some respects replaced cowardice as the central point for Henry's guilt. This is a great advance, for Henry seems more distressed by his own lack of charity than by his early dishonour. While before Henry feared that others could see his shame and know his crime of desertion, now he sees his crime as deserting this tattered man in his time of need. The tattered man, who in some respects is made a parallel figure to Jim Conklin, is different from Jim in his incisive questions.

Henry's ability not only to recall his guilt but also to manage it, humanises him and gives him hope.

Turning-points

Turning-points in the action occur when decisions are made irrevocably, so they govern a series of other actions and decisions. Perhaps one of the main turning-points in this book is the moment when Henry runs away from the battle in Chapter 6.

Others began to scamper away through the smoke. The youth turned his head, shaken from his trance by this movement as if the regiment was leaving him behind. He saw the few fleeting forms.

He yelled then with fright and swung about. For a moment, in a great clamor, he was like a proverbial chicken. He lost the direction of safety. Destruction threatened him from all points.

Directly he began to speed toward the rear in great leaps.

See if you can find at least three other turning-points in the action. Isolate the passages relating the actions involved and compare them with this critical passage. Particularly interesting is a comparison of this passage with the point at which Henry views the dead man in the forest, quoted above. Henry's points of decision show a kind of uniformity of action. Elaborate on this.

Perspective and description

Wilson and Fleming change positions, and their perspective on the battle changes. This changing perspective is a tool Crane uses to achieve the impression of wholeness in his picture of war.

> From their position as they again faced toward the place of the fighting, they could of course comprehend a greater amount of the battle than when their visions had been blurred by the hurling smoke of the line. They could see dark stretches winding along the land, and on one cleared space there was a row of guns making gray clouds, which were filled with large flashes of orange-coloured flame. Over some foliage they could see the roof of a house. One window, glowing a deep murder red, shone squarely through the leaves. From the edifice a tall leaning tower of smoke went far into the sky.
> Looking over their own troops, they saw mixed masses slowly getting into regular form. The sunlight made twinkling points of the bright steel. To the rear there was a glimpse of a distant roadway as it curved over a slope. It was crowded with retreating infantry. From all the interwoven forest arose the smoke and bluster of the battle. The air was always occupied by a blaring.   (Chapter 18)

This new perspective on the action is underscored when Wilson and Fleming overhear the general and his staff discuss the 'mule drivers' that are their regiment.

The passage quoted above is called a topographia, or description of a particular place. Notice that the whole terrain is first surveyed in broad terms. Then the roof of the house, made vivid by its window with its 'deep murder red', is focused on to bring the action within the landscape to life. Then finally the military action emerges through the landscape, with small details making the strategy clear. Sounds as well as sights are used in the description, and with the use of the words 'interwoven forest' Crane telegraphs his technique – to weave together natural elements and the war into one whole vision.

The soldier with the cheery voice

The soldier who leads Fleming back to his own regiment is identified only by the quality of his voice. Henry does not see his face or learn his name. But this figure serves as more than a mere vehicle to get Henry

from one place to another and more than a symbol of selfless charity,
though he is both. He tells a story with an unstated moral in Chapter 12:

'Yeh know there was a boy killed in my comp'ny t'-day that I thought
th' world an' all of. Jack was a nice feller. By ginger, it hurt like
thunder t' see ol' Jack jest git knocked flat. We was a-standin' purty
peaceable for a spell, 'though there was men runnin' ev'ry way all
'round us, an' while we was a-standin' like that, 'long come a big fat
feller. He began t'peck at Jack's elbow, an' he ses: "Say, where's th'
road t' th' river?" An' Jack, he never paid no attention, an' th' feller
kept on a-peckin' at his elbow an' sayin': "Say, where's th' road t' th'
river?" Jack was a lookin' ahead all th' time tryin' t' see th' Johnnies
comin' through th' woods, an' he never paid no attention t' this big
fat feller fer a long time, but at last he turned 'round an' he ses: "Ah,
go t' hell an' find th' road t' th' river!" An' jest then a shot slapped
him bang on th' side th' head. He was a sergeant, too. Them was his
last words.' (Chapter 12)

Jack, like Jimmie Rogers, is one of the faceless soldiers of report or
rumour; only the picture of his last moments is painfully complete. For
some unexplained reason the man with the cheery voice is beguiled by
the story he tells, but he draws no conclusions from it. Jack is the victim
of some sort of nemesis because of his uncharitable response to the big
fat man's question. The river and the road to it remain as mythic
fixtures in the landscape. Tom Jamison, the tattered man's friend and
neighbour, is in some respects Jack's opposite. Notice in the cheery-
voiced man's style the repetitions, which are almost incantatory,
leading to the final two short sentences. It almost seems irrelevant that
the man should add that Jack was a sergeant or that the words he
uttered were his last. It is not clear just why the man with the cheery
voice thought the world of this now-dead man. Distantly the response
Jack gives is like Henry Fleming's response to the pleas of the tattered
man, but Henry does not make the connection. The story is left as a
sort of vignette, for the reader to remember as a ghostly fragment from
the war experience.

Nature as a character

Nature, like war, is personified in the novel and almost becomes a full
character, changing as Henry's vision changes. Here is nature at a
moment of Henry's rationalisation of her in Chapter 7:

He conceived Nature to be a woman with a deep aversion to tragedy
. . . . Nature had given him a sign. The squirrel, immediately upon
recognizing danger, had taken to his legs without ado. He did not

stand stolidly baring his furry belly to the missile, and die with an upward glance at the sympathetic heavens. On the contrary, he had fled as fast as his legs could carry him; and he was but an ordinary squirrel, too – doubtless no philosopher of his race. The youth wended, feeling that Nature was of his mind. She re-enforced his arguments with proofs that lived where the sun shone.

Nature is for Henry a sympathetic woman at this point in his development. She has an aversion to tragedy, and through the squirrel she tells Henry that his flight from battle was part of the natural order. Thus he rationalises his cowardly act. Not only does nature have laws that seem to bear out Henry's fantasies but nature demonstrates those laws to him as if to soothe his troubled conscience. The problem with this train of thought, of course, is that just after the passage quoted above Henry is given another view of nature – in the dead man in the green chapel. Compare the personification of nature here as a woman with the later personification of the American flag as a woman. The word 'nature' is capitalised, as if it were a proper name. Clearly Henry's view of Nature is coloured by the gender he associates with it – femininity and sympathy are linked.

Arrangement of material

A quotation will not stand in its own defence. You must explain precisely why you use it in your argument. Use only quotations that can stand alone as grammatical units, and arrange your text to read well even if the quoted material is omitted. A quotation is like a piece of evidence at a trial. The persuasive framework makes the quotation meaningful, and the quotation, which may seem very important to you, needs to convey the same power and the same meaning to your reader. Always make sure that you quote precisely as much as you need to make your point – only that much and no more. When you begin to isolate a quotation, you are likely to discover more in it than you at first thought there was. Let the quotation guide you to deeper analysis than you had at first formulated. And be careful to do justice to the context from which you took the quotation. It does little service to your argument to distort a quotation or omit a portion just because it denies your point.

In preparing for writing a paper or an examination, you should frame likely questions to answer and then answer them with as much detail as you can. You will have to refer to events and characters with economy and accuracy, giving only enough information to refresh in your readers' minds the salient portions of the novel. In answering a question, be sure to limit yourself to that specific question. Do not get side-tracked or give so many examples that your readers tire of your argument. You will have use of the text in writing a paper, so a passive knowledge of the text is all you will need. But when sitting an examination you will need to rely on your memory of key passages to press your points. Be sure to memorise quotations that may come in handy in an essay examination.

Your answer to a question should begin with a strong statement of your own point of view. State at the outset what you intend to prove. Additionally you should set the limits of your answer and, where possible, enumerate the broad arguments that will be used to support your thesis. It is always difficult to judge exactly how much detail will be necessary to prove each point, but too much evidence is always preferable to too little.

Never equivocate in your answer. A strong answer with a few details wrong is better than a weak answer with no controlling argument to link the correct details. You cannot assume that your reader already has come to your conclusions. On the other hand, you should pay your reader the courtesy of respect for his intelligence. Possibly the best assumption is that you are writing for a good reader who has freshly encountered the work with an open mind. Your task is to give a compelling reason for the reader to evaluate what he has read and perhaps to re-read it with renewed interest. It is always a pleasure to discover that there is more to a work for you to enjoy than you first thought.

Specimen questions

These are some questions that you might pose for yourself about *The Red Badge of Courage*. Sample answers to some of the questions follow, but they are only samples. There are no 'perfect' answers, and you should be able to amplify or improve upon the answers provided.

1. Explain the irony of the major symbol 'the red badge of courage'.
2. Is war a metaphor or equivalent of life in *The Red Badge of Courage*? State why or why not.
3. Henry Fleming is a developing character in the novel. Defend or refute this statement.
4. What does the tattered man represent for Henry Fleming? How does this agree or disagree with what he represents for the reader?
5. How does Stephen Crane use nature to explore Henry Fleming's perspective on life?
6. Compare and/or contrast the friendship Fleming has with Jim Conklin to that he has with Wilson.
7. Colours have many functions in *The Red Badge of Courage*. Explore the range of functions of any one colour in the book.

8. How is the heroism of Henry Fleming comparable to that of Lieutenant Hasbrouck? How is it different?

9. What do the memories of village life contribute to Henry Fleming's views on war?

10. Is *The Red Badge of Courage* totally void of females? What, if any, is the role of women in the book?

11. Death and courage are related themes in the novel. Can you say how, and how not, these themes are related with reference to specific images of death in the work?

12. What does Crane's point of view contribute to the novel? Is his dual point of view a strength or a weakness?

13. Discuss one of these themes as it recurs through the novel: pride, betrayal, experience, illusions, entrapment, home, kindness, guilt.

14. Animal imagery in *The Red Badge of Courage* occurs on nearly every page. What animals are involved and why?

15. What are the purposes of the man with the cheery voice in the overall design of the novel?

16. Crane has been called a literary impressionist. Explain how one of these elements contributes to the impressionism of *The Red Badge of Courage*: colour, perspective, character, the war experience, description.

17. Are there any minor characters in *The Red Badge of Courage*? What is their function?

18. What allusions to the Classical literature of ancient Greece and Rome do you find in the novel? Why does Crane include them?

19. What elements contribute to the unity of the novel?

20. Henry Fleming becomes the perfect soldier and the perfect man. Say why or why not.

21. Doubling is the use of one character to bring out the traits of another by comparison or contrast or both. Fleming and Wilson are doubles. Elaborate on this.

22. Henry does a lot of thinking in the novel, but just how much do his thoughts have to do with his actions?

23. What do the stories of Tom Jamison and Jack add to the moral dimension of *The Red Badge of Courage*?

24. What is the range of meanings associated with the American flag in the novel?

25. The different levels of the military chain of command imply a succession of perspectives on the universe, each one different, and yet related to the others. Discuss the general's perspective and Henry Fleming's opinions about generals as an example.

26. Often in the novel men have difficulty communicating with each other. Explore the theme of communication in connection with its opposite, alienation, in the novel.

27. In how many ways is the literary technique of repetition used in the novel? Why?
28. What structural elements in *The Red Badge of Courage* contribute to the sense of unity achieved by the novel?
29. Compare *The Red Badge of Courage* with 'The Open Boat' or another of Crane's shorter fictional works. Discuss his attitude(s) toward nature in these works.
30. Is *The Red Badge of Courage* an epic? Defend your position.
31. If you were hiring someone to be a war correspondent, would you hire Crane on the basis of *The Red Badge of Courage*? Why?
32. What evidence in *The Red Badge of Courage* suggests that Crane may have known about the literary movement known as 'naturalism'?
33. Discuss *The Red Badge of Courage* as American propaganda.
34. How would Crane have modified *The Red Badge of Courage* if the war involved were World War II or the Vietnam War?
35. Is *The Red Badge of Courage* in any sense an answer to Melville's *Moby Dick*? How are the novels alike? How are they different?

Model answers

The answers provided for the following questions are intended to be models only, not substitutes for your own thoughts. No answer is absolute or definitive. The method of answering is at least as important as the content of the answers. The answers are in the form of essays written for a timed examination, not formal papers written and rewritten for submission with all quotations properly noted and the like. In reviewing the model answers, try to pick out the main points. Notice the means in each answer for directing the reader to the appropriate context. Also notice how each essay moves through a succession of points, each building on the preceding point until the final point is argued. Numbers of the model answers refer to the specimen questions given above.

---

1. Explain the irony of the major symbol 'the red badge of courage'.

The irony of 'the red badge of courage' is that it is initially gained while Henry Fleming is technically a deserter and coward but that it grows to become the emblem of real heroism. Like the dressing for his wound, Henry is a product of both cowardice and heroism, and one triumphant human aspect of the book is that Henry, while a hero, can be humbled by the recollection of his guilt.

Early in the story Lieutenant Hasbrouck is wounded in the hand, and his bandaged hand becomes a symbol of true heroism, pure and simple. In contrast, Henry feels after his flight from battle, past Hasbrouck, that he will always wear a badge of dishonour. Later when he joins the stream of wounded men, he feels that his guilt is written on his brow and he longs for a wound that might hide the fact that he has run away from battle. The tattered man makes such a point of wanting to know where Henry's wound is that Henry is certain that he must be discovered someday. Jim Conklin's wounded state is a constant reproach to him. Ironically, when Henry does receive his wound, it is from a man who himself is fleeing from battle. The crushing blow on Fleming's skull provides his escape and means of redemption. Not only does Henry earn the aid of the soldier with the cheery voice, but he also can rejoin his own regiment without utter dishonour. Lying about how he got the wound, he is nursed by Wilson, whose handkerchief is used as dressing for the wound.

From the time of his acceptance in camp, Fleming is sensitive to the danger of discovery, but in each engagement he proves himself worthier than before. The 'dingy rag with its spot of blood' is joined by another symbol of his worthiness – the American flag, the 'goddess, radiant'. This, an unspoiled emblem of excellence, underlines the transformation of the coward into the hero. Full of past implications with convergent themes of guilt, lying, and shame, the red badge remains an ironical symbol of courage, a reminder to Henry Fleming and the reader of the cost of heroism as well as the humility that must temper pride of achievement.

---

6. Compare and/or contrast the friendship Fleming has with Jim Conklin to that he has with Wilson.

In the opening chapter they are only the tall soldier, the loud soldier, and the youthful soldier, but already it is clear that Jim Conklin, Wilson, and Fleming are friends. Fleming is the reflective friend and can call on the resources of Conklin and Wilson; Conklin and Wilson are almost more combatants than friends. Fleming's regard for Conklin is one of great respect and affection; on the other hand, his regard for Wilson is more guarded. Where Conklin's assurance is comforting to Fleming, Wilson's fiery pride and belligerence give Henry the impression that he must be a very courageous man.

Jim Conklin is the shock awaiting Henry when he joins the stream of wounded men after his flight. Where Henry ran from battle, Jim stayed and fought and was mortally wounded. Jim recognises Henry and asks for his aid, which Henry gladly offers. Jim's death is a blow to Henry, for he has no friend to whom he is as deeply bonded. As if to emphasise the symbolism of Jim's height, Crane has him stand very tall before his final death agony brings him low, like a tree. The pathos in

Jim's death is in the reversal of the usual relation between Jim and Henry. Now Henry props Jim up, and, with the help of the tattered man, assists him, but cannot save him. Without Jim, Henry must 'go it alone'. Except for the crying need of the wounded Jim at the end, there is no development in Jim or in his relationship with Henry. The friendship is complete and whole.

In contrast, Wilson's relationship with Henry develops almost from the start. Pretending to courage in his insistence that he will not run from battle, Wilson then gives Henry the packet of papers, symbolically confessing his weakness and fear. When Henry returns from his flight experiences, he is nursed by a much changed Wilson. Where there had been hostility and detachment, there are now compassion and tenderness. Instead of causing fights, Wilson is a peacemaker, breaking them up. Wilson and Henry live and fight side by side. They share secrets, like the name 'mule drivers' or the packet which Wilson retrieves. They can still contend with each other, as over the flag, but they achieve a balanced relationship in the end. Both are congratulated by the lieutenant and colonel for their bravery, and Wilson takes the Confederate flag, just as Henry did the Union flag.

Conklin is not diminished by this comparison; rather he is ennobled. He is more a static symbol than a human and developing character. His death shows the terrible cost of war to Henry; Wilson's living allows Henry the opportunity to share his sense of achievement and it underlines by contrast Henry's means of becoming a hero.

---

14. Animal imagery in *The Red Badge of Courage* occurs on nearly every page. What animals are involved and why?

Animal imagery is used in *The Red Badge of Courage* to emphasise the inhuman brutality of war and the lowly and animal-like state of the men who find themselves in the midst of a war. The most common usage is for straight enhancement of an idea – charging like buffaloes, scolding like a wet parrot, or crawling like reptiles, but by far the most imaginative use of animals is to elaborate the symbolic structure of the novel. War is 'the red animal, war, the blood-swollen god'. Thickets seem to be porcupines with 'quills of flame'. Desires have swift wings that 'would have shattered against the iron gates of the impossible'. By accumulation, then, the allusions to animals give a sense of the inhumanity of war while the symbolic use of animals adds power to central ideas.

A full catalogue of animals referred to in the novel would run to several pages. Some of them are sheep and the animals that eat them – wolves; worms, crows, wild cats, cows, a squirrel, birds, a panther, a chicken, flies, a snake, dragons, a rabbit, hounds, a dog, a kitten, pigs, eagles and so on. Most of these are used to represent a characteristic quality of the soldiers. In triumph the soldiers fly like eagles; when they are marched or driven into battle, they are sheep. Perhaps worse than being animals for Wilson and Fleming is being accused of driving them – 'mule drivers' is the ultimate insult. For Henry the enemy are dragons, and it is a comfort to him to discover that the dragons do not always 'sting with precision'. When Henry is described as having 'a certain mothlike quality' that keeps him in the vicinity of the battle, the animal imagery becomes involved with symbol, for the unconscious drive towards glory and the threat of death is at the centre of Henry's will. When he is like the proverbial chicken at the time of flight, this theme is also present.

Animal imagery becomes highly symbolic in such powerful scenes as when Henry, far from battle, discovers the dead Union soldier in the little woodland sanctuary. There the staring eye is the colour of a dead fish's. Ants that crawl over the grey face are black and seem unconcerned that this thing was once a man. Nature's unconcern for man, even her possession of the dead, is underlined by the use of animal imagery. In the encounters with Jim Conklin and the tattered man the lamblike qualities of both add to the pathos. Jim's side looks as if it had been torn by wolves; the tattered man does not talk as much as bleat. These are war's sacrifices. Throughout, the insistent image of war as 'the red animal' subsumes all other animal images in the terrifying gobbling and insatiable god. The dragons of the enemy are not the threat that war itself is. Man's attempts within this larger animal framework seem only dimly reflective of the larger symbol. Animal imagery intimately relates the little conflicts of men to the larger idea of war itself.

---

23. What do the stories of Tom Jamison and Jack add to the moral dimension of *The Red Badge of Courage*?

Among the numerous minor characters in the novel, Tom and Jack stand out because they are mentioned after Jim Conklin's moving death. The tattered soldier mentions his neighbour and fellow soldier Tom Jamison by way of explaining how he came to be wounded twice; the soldier with the cheery voice tells the tale of Jack as he directs Henry back to camp. It is somewhat ironical that these two nameless and somewhat symbolic soldiers should etch with clarity stories about named soldiers whose actions take place out of the vision of Henry or the reader. Both stories have moral meaning, and the meaning of each acts as a contrast to the other, though they are related in that both involve an interchange between two men and both involve insensitivity to the needs of others.

Tom Jamison, the tattered man's neighbour back home, tells the tattered man when he has been hit in the head. Otherwise oblivious of this fact, the tattered man then runs in panic and only then is hit by another bullet in the arm. The tattered man now thinks he might still be fighting if Jamison had not told him about his head wound. Because he respected Jamison for his intelligence and affected superiority, he lost his head and ran when Jamison shouted and cursed him for his head wound. In his delirium, the tattered man identifies Henry Fleming with Tom Jamison, and without being conscious of it, implicates Henry in the same sort of insensitivity that Jamison had.

Jack, a friend of the man with the cheery voice, is a sergeant who, when approached in battle by a man who wants to know the way to the road to the river, at first ignores him and then, annoyed at his pestering, tells him to go to hell to find it. At that moment of uncharitableness, the unlucky Jack is struck in the head by a bullet that kills him instantly. The man with the cheery voice offers no interpretation of the incident. Ironically the enemy he sought with such concentration found him at the precise moment when he dropped his guard.

The two incidents are linked by Tom's and Jack's inability at a moment of crisis to act with instinctive kindness. For Tom the rash outburst causes the second wound and possibly also the death of his neighbour. For Jack, although the causal connection is left unclear, his lack of charity is followed by his own death. Clearly also both incidents have profoundly influenced the two men who tell the tales. The tattered soldier does not want Henry Fleming (whom he confuses with Tom Jamison) to go away from him because he wants to give the kindness his friend withheld. The man with the cheery voice may also be motivated in his kindness to Henry by the image of Jack's death. The two stories underline, if not the morality of wounds and death in war, at least the transforming power of human actions on those who witness them.

Part 5

Suggestions for further reading

The text

CRANE, STEPHEN: *The Red Badge of Courage*, Appleton and Company, New York, 1895. The first American edition. This does not include, of course, the manuscript material.

The Red Badge of Courage, ed. by Wilson Follett, in *The Works of Stephen Crane,* 12 vols., Knopf, New York, 1925-7. This complete edition of the works was superseded by the Virginia edition cited below.

The Red Badge of Courage, ed. by John T. Winterich, The Folio Society, London, 1951. This contains the first reproduction of the final manuscript of *The Red Badge of Courage,* but is incomplete and erroneous.

Stephen Crane: An Omnibus, ed. by R. W. Stallman, Knopf, New York, 1952; Heinemann, London, 1954. Includes two manuscripts of *The Red Badge of Courage.*

The Red Badge of Courage and Selected Prose and Poetry, ed. by William M. Gibson, Rinehart, New York, 1956. The text is the same as in the faulty Winterich edition above.

The Red Badge of Courage and Other Stories, ed. by Daniel G. Hoffman, Harper's Modern Classics, New York, 1957.

The Red Badge of Courage and Selected Stories, ed. by R. W. Stallman, New American Library, New York, 1960. The Signet edition, claimed to be definitive.

The Red Badge of Courage and Other Stories, with an introduction by V. S. Pritchett and a note on the texts by R. W. Stallman, Oxford University Press, London, 1960, paperback 1969.

The Red Badge of Courage, ed. by Fredson Bowers, in *The Works of Stephen Crane,* 10 vols., University Press of Virginia, Charlottesville, Virginia, 1969-75, Vol. 2. The Virginia edition of Crane supersedes all previous editions. It includes every known piece of his creative writing and journalism, except his letters and memoranda; but beware – this 'definitive' text has been criticised by Donald Pizer and others.

The Red Badge of Courage, ed. by Donald Pizer, W. W. Norton and Co., New York, 1976. The Norton Critical Edition with complete apparatus and critical commentary.

Also see:

The Stephen Crane Reader, Scott, Foresman, and Company, Glenville, Illinois, 1972. Contains reproductions of the text of the first American edition, the shorter manuscript version (SV) and longer manuscript version (LV) and five pages of additional manuscript from various libraries.

Biography

BEER, THOMAS: *Stephen Crane: A Study in American Letters,* Garden City, New York, 1923.

BERRYMAN, JOHN: *Stephen Crane,* World Publishing Company, Cleveland, 1950; repr. Octagon, New York, 1970.

GILKES, LILLIAN: *Cora Crane: A Biography of Mrs. Stephen Crane,* University of Indiana, Bloomington, Indiana, 1960.

STALLMAN, R. W.: *Stephen Crane: A Biography,* G. Braziller, New York, 1968.

Bibliography

GROSS, THEODORE and WERTHEIM, STANLEY: *Hawthorne, Melville, Stephen Crane: A Critical Biography,* Free Press, New York, 1971.

KATZ, JOSEPH: 'Afterword: Resources for the Study of Stephen Crane', in Katz's edition of *Centenary Essays* below, under 'Collections of critical essays'.

PIZER, DONALD: 'Stephen Crane', in Robert A. Rees and E. N. Harbert (eds.), *Fifteen American Authors Before 1900: Bibliographical Essays on Research and Criticism,* University of Wisconsin Press, Madison, Wisconsin, 1971.

STALLMAN, R. W.: *Stephen Crane: A Critical Bibliography,* Iowa State University Press, Ames, 1972.

Criticism

BARGON, FRANK: *Stephen Crane's Artistry,* Columbia University Press, New York, 1975.

CADY, EDWIN H.: *Stephen Crane,* rev. edn., Twayne Publishers, Boston, 1980. A good introduction to Crane.

HOFFMAN, DANIEL G.: *The Poetry of Stephen Crane,* Columbia University Press, New York, 1957.

LA FRANCE, MARSTON: *A Reading of Stephen Crane,* Clarendon Press, Oxford, 1971.

NAGEL, JAMES: *Stephen Crane and Literary Impressionism,* University of Pennsylvania Press, University Park, Pennsylvania, 1980.

SOLOMON, ERIC: *Stephen Crane: From Parody to Realism,* Harvard University Press, Cambridge, Massachusetts, 1966.

Collections of critical essays

BASSAN, M. (ED.): *Stephen Crane: A Collection of Critical Essays,* Prentice-Hall, Englewood Cliffs, New Jersey, 1967.

GULLASON, THOMAS A. (ED.): *Stephen Crane's Career: Perspectives and Evaluations,* New York University Press, New York, 1972.

KATZ, JOSEPH (ED.): *Stephen Crane in Transition: Centenary Essays,* Northern Illinois University Press, Dekalb, 1972.

PARKER, HERSHEL (ED.): 'Special Number on Stephen Crane', *Studies in the Novel,* 10, Spring, 1978, 182 pp.

WEATHERFORD, RICHARD M. (ED.): *Stephen Crane: The Critical Heritage,* Routledge and Kegan Paul, London and Boston, 1973. Limited to commentaries made during Crane's lifetime and just afterward.

The author of these notes

WILSON F. ENGEL is a graduate of the University of Wisconsin–Madison; he has held teaching posts at the University of Wisconsin–Richland Center, at the University of Edinburgh, and Allentown College. He has written various articles and his edition of James Shirley's *The Gentleman of Venice* was published in 1976. He is also the author of the York Notes on *Quentin Durward* and *Moby Dick*.

The first 250 titles

The first ten titles

YORK HANDBOOKS form a companion series to York Notes and are designed to meet the wider needs of students of English and related fields. Each volume is a compact study of a given subject area, written by an authority with experience in communicating the essential ideas to students of all levels.

AN INTRODUCTORY GUIDE TO ENGLISH LITERATURE
by MARTIN STEPHEN

PREPARING FOR EXAMINATIONS IN ENGLISH LITERATURE
by NEIL McEWAN

AN INTRODUCTION TO LITERARY CRITICISM
by RICHARD DUTTON

THE ENGLISH NOVEL
by IAN MILLIGAN

ENGLISH POETRY
By CLIVE T. PROBYN

STUDYING CHAUCER
by ELISABETH BREWER

STUDYING SHAKESPEARE
by MARTIN STEPHEN *and* PHILIP FRANKS

ENGLISH USAGE
by COLIN G. HEY

A DICTIONARY OF LITERARY TERMS
by MARTIN GRAY

READING THE SCREEN
An Introduction to Film Studies
by JOHN IZOD